APPOINTMENT
IN AREZZO

APPOINTMENT IN AREZZO

A Friendship with Muriel Spark

ALAN TAYLOR

Polygon

First published in Great Britain in 2017 by
Polygon, an imprint of Birlinn Ltd

West Newington House
10 Newington Road
Edinburgh
EH9 1QS

www.polygonbooks.co.uk

ISBN: 978 1 84697 375 8

British Library Cataloguing-in-Publication Data
A catalogue record for this book is available on request from the British Library

Designed and typeset by Teresa Monachino
Printed and bound in Britain by T J International Ltd, Padstow

CONTENTS

Piazza Grande, Arezzo

INTRODUCTION

I may take up detective work one of these days.
It would be quite my sort of thing.

THE COMFORTERS

I had an appointment with Muriel Spark in Arezzo, the Tuscan town where Vasari, fabled for his *Lives* of the Renaissance artists, was born and bred. Mrs Spark's fax was brief and business-like. 'My friend Penelope Jardine and I will come to Arezzo. I suggest we have dinner there at the Continentale Hotel (not far from the station) and we can talk then. Daytimes are very hot.'

The month was July, the year 1990, and only mad dogs and impatient tourists dared expose themselves to the unforgiving sun. During the mid-afternoon, when Spark's working day habitually began, I hid in the hotel and watched an Italian soap opera on television. At six o'clock I took a stroll and by no grand design ended up at Vasari's house in a shaded back street in the *centro storico*. The house was cool, palatial, and empty save for the mute custodian who followed me from room to room with the air of someone who suspected something fishy was afoot.

In that place and at that time, the connection between Spark and Vasari seemed obvious. A fairly pious Catholic and a patriot whose allegiance was to the Medicis, Giorgio Vasari divorced himself from the religious and political issues of his day; art was his obsession. Of course, no one with even a passing acquaintance with her work would say that Spark was oblivious to great world events. On the contrary, they inform her fiction to an extraordinary if subterranean degree. From the rise of Fascism in *The Prime of Miss Jean Brodie* to her satire of the Watergate scandal, *The Abbess of Crewe*, she was always aware of what was going on in the world at large. But she was never flatly topical: no one with her intellectual attitude to faith and its implications for the hereafter could be. Like Fleur Talbot, her alter ego in *Loitering with Intent*, her sense of herself as an artist was absolute: 'That I was a woman and living in the 20th century were plain facts. That I was an artist was a conviction so strong that I never thought of doubting it then or since.' Even when Fleur makes love her mind is elsewhere, despite efforts to think of General de Gaulle. How like Vasari's hero, Uccello, droning on about the beauties of perspective while his wife tries to drag him bedwards.

In the Piazza Guido Monaco, the *Aretini* had come out to play. Old men, gnarled as walnuts, dealt cards while their sons drank beer and their grandsons harassed pigeons. Growling motor bikes raced round the square at intemperate speed. 'There is carnage every night on the roads of Italy,' observed Muriel – as she will now be called – matter-of-factly. She was a mite early for our appointment and in phrase book Italian ordered a gin and tonic while Penelope Jardine – Penny – parked their car. They had been together for twenty years, sharing a rambling house deep in the Val di Chiana, fifteen kilometres from Arezzo. Centuries ago the house, which is attached to a parish church, had been inhabited by a priest who added rooms as necessity determined. Two separate families had lived in it with the priest and his mother, some twenty people in all. Now it offered books a home, roughly seven thousand of them. 'I buy books,' said Muriel penitentially, 'I often advertise for books; I spend a fortune. I do need rare books from time to time. We have endless encyclopaedias.'

The two women seemed comfortable together, often ending each other's sentences, one deferring to the other when she couldn't put a finger on a fact or recollect a date. The notion that Muriel was some kind of recluse or eccentric, as at least one ill-informed journalist had suggested, seemed absurd. Similarly, the idea of two women living together had raised prurient eyebrows. But why should it? Penny is a sculptor who has exhibited at the Royal Academy in London; she supplied the domestic and business circumstances which allowed Muriel to flourish. 'Penny provides Muriel with emotional security,' someone who knew them both told me.

Enough emotional security to be flirting at seventy-two. I mentioned that I had tried with just a few words of Italian at my command to buy trousers in Florence. If I had told her that I'd been diagnosed with a terminal illness she couldn't have shown more concern. 'Let's ask that dishy waiter who is the best *sarto* in Arezzo.' While the man was summoned, Muriel asked if my hair was as nature intended. It was, I confessed. 'You don't do anything to it? Touch it up?' I said I paid a man called Alfie in Edinburgh to keep it out of my eyes and off my collar. 'I never touch up mine either,' she trumped.

As the waiter was interrogated about the best tailor in town I took the opportunity to study Muriel. She looked at least ten years younger than her age. Her hair, touched up or not, was red, as it was when she was a girl growing up in Edinburgh and before it was bleached under Rhodesian skies when she was in her early twenties. She was petite, with a gay and curious demeanour. She seemed to me someone to whom you could talk unguardedly, like a doctor or a priest, without fear of it ever being passed on. She dressed elegantly and expensively. Her dress was a riot of yellow and black. Round her neck she wore a string of white pearls and a canary-yellow silk scarf. She had a reputation for being waspish, once making mincemeat of a BBC interviewer who asked a fatuous question. When I told her – sincerely – how much I admired her latest book, *Symposium*, her dark eyes lit up and her face creased with pleasure.

The life of a 'constitutional exile' appeared to suit her. No one, though, should be deceived into thinking that the road to Arezzo had been straight and smooth. At that time, her autobiography, *Curriculum Vitae*, had yet to appear. When it did – in 1992 – it ended with the publication in 1957 of her first novel, *The Comforters*, just as her career as a writer was beginning. At thirty-nine she was a relatively late starter, but, as she makes plain in the autobiography, her life up to that point was about laying foundations and accumulating experience. 'Since I wrote my first novel,' she stated towards the end of *Curriculum Vitae*, 'I have passed the years occupied with ever more work, many travels and adventures. Friends, famous and obscure, abound in my life-story. That will be the subject of another volume.'

That promised volume never materialised. In Arezzo, Muriel was happy to revisit her distant past, which was full of obscure people, some of whom had subsequently gained prominence because of their association with her. She was born on 1 February, 1918, while the 'war to end all wars' was still rumbling on. She told me her brother, Philip, who was five years older than her, had had a distinguished career as an engineer with Boeing in California. We talked about her father, Bertie Camberg, a Jew who was born in Scotland and who ran away to sea when he was fourteen. 'He got as far as Kirkwall.' Her mother was English and an Anglican. There was no hint of gypsy blood in her, she remarked, countering a falsehood first spread by Derek Stanford, a former lover and collaborator.

A memoir he had written had infuriated her and continued to cause her anxiety because it was often quoted. He was one of the reasons why she had embarked on *Curriculum Vitae*. 'He is the limit,' she said, her voice rising an octave. 'He was very fond of me. Absolutely. But as soon as I got any form of success he went so sour. He sold all my letters to Texas University. Then he started writing books full of the wildest things about my life, and the whole thing I ignored. I never did a thing. I am much too busy and life is too short. However, I thought I would put the record straight. One critic picks it up and then another and on it goes. He's a mythomaniac.'

Bertie Camberg was an engineer with the North British Rubber Works. He was a betting man, fond of horse-racing, an interest his daughter inherited; at one time Muriel had a share in two racehorses, neither of which was conspicuously successful. Her mother, Sarah, she reckoned, could have been a Bruntsfield Madame Bovary. 'Quite easily,' she said. 'She was craving for what she called the "bright lights".' In *Curriculum Vitae* she recreated in meticulous and loving detail the first five years of her life, a whiff of Nivea cream being the equivalent of Proust's *petite madeleine*. 'Sometimes', she wrote, 'I compare my early infancy with that of my friends whose very early lives were in the hands of nannies, and who were surrounded by servants and privilege. Those pre-school lives seem nothing like so abundant as mine was, nothing like so crammed with people and with amazing information. I was not set aside from adult social life, nor cosied up in a nursery, and taken for nice regular walks far from the madding crowd. I was witness to the whole passing scene. Perhaps no other life could ever be as rich as that first life, when, five years old, prepared and briefed to my full capacity, I was ready for school.'

Muriel at her first meeting with Alan Taylor in Arezzo, 1990

In the 1920s and 1930s, Edinburgh, Scotland's precipitous capital, was a provincial, culturally inward, begrimed city. To a dyspeptic observer, such as the poet Edwin Muir, it was a city of 'extraordinary and sordid contrasts'. It is true, and something of a cliché, that it was a divided city, in which Robert Louis Stevenson's novella *The Strange Case of Dr Jekyll and Mr Hyde* was conceived, where wealth and poverty were bedmates. The air in Spark's teenage years was sweet with the smell from the numerous breweries. *Haars* – bone-chilling mists – rolled in from the Firth of Forth to the north of the city, and the wind, which so discomfited Stevenson, seemed never to cease blowing. Edinburgh was a city of lawyers and accountants, clergymen and teachers, of pen-pushers who made a living without getting dirt under their nails.

As a child, Muriel was aware of what she called 'social nervousness'. Though Edinburgh was not the worst-hit of Britain's major cities during the depression in the 1930s it was impossible to avoid the gulf between the haves and the have nots. Men and women queued for welfare payments, and ex-servicemen, veterans of the First World War, busked in the streets. In *The Prime of Miss Jean Brodie*, the teacher's favoured girls, the crème de la crème, are taken on a walk through Edinburgh's Old Town, with its cobbled streets, dark, narrow alleyways – known locally as closes – and vertiginous tenements, built long before Manhattan's skyscrapers were conceived. It is alien territory for the girls, 'because none of their parents was so historically minded as to be moved to conduct their young into the reeking network of slums which the Old Town constituted in those years'. This was a part of Edinburgh that just over a century earlier had been abandoned by the upwardly mobile and the gentry who, discomfited by overcrowding and noxious odours which were a result of the inhabitants dumping

Muriel, aged 10, in Edinburgh, where she was first 'understood'

their waste in the street, had fled to what was, and is, known as the New Town. Where once dwelt the aristocracy now there were 'the idle'.

For Muriel, who lived on the city's south side in a middle-class enclave, in close proximity to hills and with an abundance of street life on her doorstep, Edinburgh was where she was first 'understood'. The school she attended – James Gillespie's High School for Girls – was formative and was to be immortalised as

Marcia Blaine School in *The Prime of Miss Jean Brodie*, becoming almost as famous as St Trinian's and Dotheboys Hall. Looking back, Muriel saw that it was 'more progressive' than she realised. Her schooldays were 'very pleasant, very enjoyable'. Recalling Jean Brodie echoing the boast of the Jesuits – 'Give me a girl at an impressionable age, and she is mine for life' – she asked herself if a bad teacher could have killed her interest in writing and literature. She was adamant in her response. 'No. I'd have written at home.' Her first poem appeared in a school magazine when she was nine, and one appeared annually until the school broke its own rule and published five in the same year by the precocious student who regarded herself as 'the school's poet and dreamer'. With this status came 'appropriate perquisites and concessions'. In 1970, she wrote: 'I took this for granted, and have never since quite accustomed myself to the world's indifference to art and the process of art, and to the special needs of artists.'

She lived in Edinburgh until she was nineteen. In an oft-quoted passage, written in a hotel where she waited as her father lay dying, she wrote: 'It was Edinburgh that bred within me the conditions of exile; and what have I been doing since but moving from exile to exile. It has ceased to be a fate, it has become a calling.' For her, exile was not a negative condition but something she embraced, allowing her the freedom and space and distance to write. Away from Edinburgh and Scotland, away from anywhere in which she felt constricted and obligated and misunderstood, she could work untrammelled. In that sense, her ethic was Presbyterian: Life is what you make of it. What one achieved was by one's efforts. Take nothing for granted. Expect no favours – nor, for that matter, much in the way of thanks or praise.

Muriel left her homeland because she had met a man with whom she believed herself in love. In her teens, she said, she was constantly falling in love. Over supper in Arezzo, she told me: 'My best love affairs were when I was young – eighteen, nineteen – and I was surrounded by students. I had a really nice time then. But I had to be in – home – early.' Surrounded by students she may have been but she did not go to university. It was certainly not for lack of academic collateral. Money, or rather the lack of it, was undoubtedly a factor. Looking back on those years, however, Muriel regarded university as something of a luxury and a waste of precious time. Other, older, girls who went to university, she noticed, seemed dull and earnest and gauche, lacking charm, one of her favourite words and a quality she prized. So what if these girls could write an essay on John Donne – so could she. Nevertheless she took a course in précis-writing at Heriot-Watt College, now a university, schooling her early in finding the briefest way to express meaning. Few writers have been as parsimonious with words as she. Fewer still have written such short books layered with significance. Often, she'd jokingly remark, she felt she was short-changing her readers, so slim were her novels. Fleur in *Loitering with Intent* spoke for her when she said: 'I've come to learn for myself how little one needs, in the art of writing, to convey the lot, and how a lot of words, on the other hand, can convey so little.' What Muriel was doing in those apprentice days was very practically and conscientiously banking the skills and the wherewithal she would need when she became a writer. In order to write about life, as she intended to do, she had first to learn to live. Among the other subjects she studied were shorthand and typing, both of which she later found to be highly useful. Thus she learned how to style letters and to present essays and stories. As a professional eavesdropper, she was well aware of how handy it was for future reference to be able quickly to take shorthand notes of 'meetings, encounters, chance remarks overheard on a train, in a restaurant'. *Pace* Isherwood, she was a camera with its shutter forever open.

With each new month her horizons expanded. She longed to work in Princes Street, then, as today, Edinburgh's main, mile-long shopping thoroughfare, on the north side of which were large department stores, each independently owned. On the south side loomed Edinburgh Castle perched atop a volcanic plug, simultaneously a symbol of impregnability and paranoia. Getting a job proved difficult, not, she was eager to emphasise, because her Camberg surname marked her out as a Jew and therefore a target of anti-Semitism, but because of her lack of experience and secretarial qualifications. Eventually she was taken on by William Small and Sons, one of the more modish Edinburgh fashion emporia. It suited her perfectly. Her employer was sweet and old-fashioned and she was allowed to help him choose fabrics, always urging on him the bolder designs, a taste that never left her. He was also a source of folk wisdom, of which she was an avid collector. 'The majority of old people die in November,' was one of his many aperçus.

Little by little, she was liberating herself; she was hungry to discover what lay beyond Edinburgh and its environs. Just how desperate she was to leave may be gauged by the manner in which she achieved it. At nineteen, in 1937, when war was so close you could almost touch it, she agreed to marry Sydney Oswald Spark, a teacher who was thirteen years her senior. Was she in love? I asked. 'Not madly, no, but I thought it was nice to get away.' In her autobiography, she recalled that several of her friends were engaged to be married. Perhaps that was why she was so keen to do the same. What her friends were not doing, though, was leaving Edinburgh for a new life in Rhodesia, which we now know as Zimbabwe. Her parents, in particular her father, disapproved of her husband-to-be, but to no avail. How could she turn her back on a man who brought her flowers when she was in bed with flu? The marriage was an unmitigated disaster. With the benefit of hindsight she made her personal motto, 'Beware of men bearing flowers.' 'I was only married a short time,' she said, as the sun sank over Arezzo and the sky turned black and blue like a bruise. 'Love is madness. There is nothing you can do about it. You must wait till it passes; it's like any other obsession.'

Muriel in Rhodesia in 1940. Her parents disapproved of her husband

The same is probably true of pain. Sixty years on, the scars of her marriage to 'S.O.S.' had healed but were still noticeable. On that first meeting we did not talk much about it. In *Curriculum Vitae*, she related how in Rhodesia her husband began to show the first signs of a nervous disorder that would haunt him for the rest of his life. Immediately after their son, Robin, was born she realised the marriage was doomed, and she sought a divorce. Since her husband wouldn't divorce her, she divorced him. But she retained his surname. Camberg, she reasoned, was 'comparatively flat'. In contrast, Spark had a bit of oomph about it, a bit of get up and go. It was an affirming, memorable surname. Moreover, it seemed to sum up her personality: no one was ever more sparky than Muriel Spark. That much was clear on that evening in Arezzo. The popular image of her was of someone who rather resented the world and was something of a misanthrope. Nothing was further from the truth, as her novels testify. What she would concede was that, whenever she felt her ability to write was in any way compromised, she had to retreat, to remove herself from temptation and supplication, from the hangers-on, pub bores and spongers, who would cling to her like leeches, whether in London, where she lived in the aftermath of war, New York, or Rome. She drew an analogy with the forest fires that sweep Tuscany in the summer months. To prevent these spreading, the local people make a *contra fuoco*, a counter-fire round the perimeter of the fire. 'They say, "So far and no farther. That fire is raging and devouring. It won't get past this stretch because it's burnt down." And I think that's what I've had to do with my life; make a counter-fire, to stop the encroachment of really devouring demands.' Thus she had managed to avoid the many 'enemies of promise'. The pram in the hall did not thwart her, as it has many women writers, nor did sex, success, sloth or self-doubt. Regarding her vocation, she was unswerving.

Symposium's title is borrowed from Plato's dialogue, in which guests at a banquet take it in turn to talk about love – mythically, sophistically, poetically and, finally, comically. Socrates said that the priestess Diotima had taught him that it was possible for love to take an intellectual form, creating the desire to make things of beauty, including poetry. Set partly in London and Scotland, *Symposium* has as one of its themes madness. 'Here in Scotland', says Magnus Murchie, 'people are more capable of perpetrating good or evil than anywhere else. I don't know why, but so it is.' The Murchies live in 'a turreted edifice' near the golfing Mecca of St Andrews, a game which Muriel played on Bruntsfield links when she was young. Magnus is mad, but during periodic bouts of lucidity he is allowed out of the mental institution to advise his family on how they should run their affairs. When one of them questions the wisdom of this, Magnus retorts:

> Who do you have but me? Out of my misfortune, out of my affliction I prognosticate and foreshadow. My divine affliction is your only guide. Remember the ballad:
>
>> As I went down the water side
>> None but my foe to be my guide
>> None but my foe to be my guide.

Muriel remembered the Border ballads from her youth and could recite large chunks of them by heart. They are remarkable for their sense of fatality and lack of sentimentality. The most awful things are reported matter-of-factly, needing no embroidery. Death and misfortune are not occasions for lachrymosity. They speak for themselves.

'What do you think of Magnus?' Muriel asked. I muttered something inadequate, perhaps suggesting that it was stretching credulity somewhat to have a madman as a familial mentor. 'It's amazing how many people do go to bins [lunatic asylums], or to their mad relations,' she countered, 'especially in Scotland.' Over the intervening years I have often pondered that remark and have grown to accept its truth. Certainly, the Scotland that Muriel grew up in was remarkable for its acceptance of 'lunatics', of whom even the smallest town had a smattering, some 'barking', others merely oddly behaved. Who knows why there was such a preponderance? Hellfire-and-damnation religion? Generations of inbreeding? The constant harping on about ghosts and ghouls, witches and warlocks? What is undeniable is that in Muriel's work real and other worlds exist in tandem, as naturally as human beings and animals.

Though it was many years since she had left Scotland Muriel still spoke with a pronounced accent. It hurt her, she said, to think that anyone might think her other than Scottish. 'What are you if you're not Scottish?' Penny interjected while we were still at the table. In Scotland, there is a tendency to measure one's Scottishness as if it were weighed in carats. Scots who live outside the country of their birth live in constant danger of deracination.

We left the Continentale and stepped into the Tuscan dusk, and Muriel and her chauffeuse set off on their journey home. I bought a glass of chianti in the piazza. I opened Vasari at his life of Brunelleschi, who built Florence's famous *Duomo*, among other wonders. Swap genders and he could have been talking about Muriel Spark: 'Many men are created by nature small in person and in features, who have a mind full of such greatness and a heart of such irresistible vehemence, that if they do not begin difficult – nay, almost impossible – undertakings, and bring them to completion to the marvel of all who behold them, they have never any peace in their lives . . .'

A few weeks after my article based on the interview in Arezzo appeared in the newspaper for which I then worked I received a complimentary letter from Penny, gently correcting a couple of errors and asking if I would be interested in looking after their house the following summer. It was put in such a way that I was made to feel I was doing them a favour. How could one refuse? Now Spark magically metamorphosed into Muriel. It was the overture to a friendship which continued until her death, and which included the exchange of many letters and phone calls, frequent sojourns in Tuscany, trips to New York, London, Prague and, finally, in 2004, to Scotland and Edinburgh. Muriel was an inveterate traveller, never happier than when climbing into the passenger seat of the Alfa Romeo and motoring thousands of miles. In 1995, I helped make a BBC documentary about her. What, I asked in a preparatory letter, was her achievement, her legacy? 'I have realised myself,' she wrote. 'I have expressed something I brought into the world with me. I believe I have liberated the novel in many ways, showing how anything whatsoever can be narrated, any experience set down, including sheer damn cheek. I think I have opened doors and windows in the mind, and challenged fears – especially the most inhibiting fears about what a novel should be.' As for her roots, her origins, her nationality, she said simply this: 'I am Scottish by formation.'

The front door of the church adjoining San Giovanni

1

SAN GIOVANNI

There was a heatwave so fierce you would have thought someone had
turned it on somewhere by means of a tap, and had turned it too
high, and then gone away for the summer.

THE TAKEOVER

The Italian public holiday known as Ferragosto falls in the middle of August and coincides with the feast of the Assumption of Mary. In the 1920s, when Fascism was in the ascendant, the regime organised holidays to the coast or the countryside for families who would otherwise be unable to afford them. Uppermost in the minds of many folk is a desire to find a bolt-hole fanned by a breeze. Even for natives the heat is enervating and places that would normally be inundated with day-trippers can seem like ghost towns.

We arrived – my then wife Rene and I and our two children, Michael, aged ten, and Jennifer, aged eight – at Florence by rail from Edinburgh not long after the sun had risen and the cool of the night was giving way to what promised to be a broiling day. As the train crept caterpillar-like into Santa Maria Novella station I spied an old woman, her skin brown and leathery, her belongings stuffed into plastic bags, sluicing herself vigorously at a tap on a platform. She was naked from the waist up, her breasts as flat and empty as her purse. As she looked up she smiled toothlessly and unselfconsciously, as if her routine was one of the city's many draws. I waved back for it felt like a welcoming omen. *'Buon giorno,'* the topless dame mouthed and returned to her ablutions.

Florence – the City of Flowers – was wakening. Even inside the station's concourse you could hear the melancholy peal of a bell calling the faithful to morning mass. With a few hours to spare before we were expected at Arezzo we surrendered our bags to the surly custodians of the Deposito Bagagli and stepped into the sunlight. The first thing one noticed was the stench, which was of a cocktail of drains, decomposing fruit and vegetables and the throat-grasping ordure of horses who stood outside the Duomo, engrossed in nosebags while their chain-smoking handlers waited for the first tourists to abandon their hotels. There were only a few cars, most of them taxis. The streets were narrow and winding, and the tall buildings, with their thick walls, stout oak doors and ornate, steel-barred windows, spoke of a past when repelling intruders was uppermost in the minds of their inhabitants. It took no great effort to imagine the city in a ferment of construction and creativity at the height of the Renaissance. You could feel it coming alive and opening up. In *A Room with a View*, E. M. Forster talks of Italy's 'pernicious charm', and I first felt its effect that luminous morning as the sun's restorative rays began to alight on the smooth, foot-polished flagstones and marble benches.

We headed in the direction of Piazza della Signoria where for breakfast and as a reward for model behaviour on the two-day-long journey the children had been promised ice-cream as their first introduction to foreign climes and customs. On the opposite side of the square rose the Palazzo Vecchio in which the fanatical friar Savonarola – he who had stopped Botticelli painting – had been imprisoned and tortured before being hanged and burned just a few feet from where we were guzzling *gelato*. Here we were in the heart of the capital of culture. A stone's throw away, too, was the Uffizi Gallery, beyond which the languid Arno flowed beneath the Ponte Vecchio, the only Florentine bridge which Adolf Hitler could not bring himself to blow to smithereens. On the other, south side of the river – Oltrarno – were the Boboli Gardens and the gargantuan Pitti Palace, which Arnold Bennett likened to a military barracks.

There was nothing unremarkable about Florence. It was almost too much to take in; sightseeing, in any case, would have to wait until later. Shutters banged ajar and elderly women stuck out their heads and beckoned to neighbours who were already en route to market to have their pick of the freshest produce. At a decibel level that would have roused the entombed, the music of the language was apparent even to our children. From alleyways emerged traders bent double dragging their ingeniously designed carts which, on opening, became stalls selling the gamut of leather goods. It was a scene that made one think of stories of the American West in which poor immigrants pulled their covered wagons across uncharted land in the hope that somewhere over the horizon a better life awaited.

Save for the vaporous trail left by a jet, the sky was a uniform blue. While the children harried pigeons in the square I fished out the letter Penny had sent a year or so earlier inviting us to look after her house while she and Muriel would be travelling elsewhere. She had read my interview with Muriel and felt that it might be a case of 'blood speaking to blood', meaning, I supposed, our shared Scottish roots. 'It is very good news that you may seriously mean to come here next August,' she continued. 'It will mean a lot to us, especially for Muriel who likes to keep a cool head when writing, and to me especially to think above all that intelligent people are in charge of my house and I hope enjoying it.'

There was no charge, Penny emphasised, for all of this. What she and Muriel were especially glad of was that their animals – two dogs and 'some' outside cats – would be well looked after, that the house would be occupied and that its contents would be protected. Muriel's half of the house would be locked up; we would have the run of the rest, including bedrooms, bathrooms, living rooms and the kitchen. We would not need to worry about bed linen, and there were books and music aplenty to keep us amused. There had been a recent drought in Italy but of late it had rained so there ought not to be a problem with water. In any case, the house had its own well. Nearby was a swimming pool, a discotheque, reputedly the largest in Europe, and a supermarket. The view, Penny concluded, was exceptional, taking in the Apennines, the Val di Chiana, Cortona, Lake Trasimeno and, on clear days, Orvieto. Rome, however, remained out of sight. 'All of August we will keep for you and your family.'

I thought of John Mortimer's recently published novel *Summer's Lease*, in which an English family rent a villa in the hills of 'Chiantishire' for the summer. All that was missing from Penny's description was the warning given to the Pargeters that, 'those alarmed by insect life should consider holidaying in Skegness'. Shortly before our departure Penny had also sent a map which she had drawn on two sides of A4 in the mistaken belief that we would be arriving by car. In itself it was a work of art but over the many years that I have made the short journey from Arezzo to San Giovanni in Oliveto I have come also to appreciate its topographical accuracy.

San Giovanni, the house in which Muriel and Penny lived, is situated below the small hill town of Civitella. It is on what is known as a *strada bianca*, a white, tarmac-free road more

Muriel and Penelope Jardine at Civitella in the late 1980s. They first met in a hairdresser's in Rome

suited to hikers and mountain bikers than cars which, even when driven at snail's pace, whip up clouds of dust. It was by chance, 'not choice', that Muriel said she had come to live here. She first visited the house that was to become her last home in the mid-1970s when she was writing *The Takeover*, which, unusually for her, was proving difficult to complete. Ever generous, Penny invited her to stay. 'I moved in for a few weeks and have remained ever since,' recalled Muriel many years later. Until then she had shown little affinity with the countryside and its remoteness from urban comfort and convenience. Initially, she was accepted by her Tuscan neighbours with 'a certain reserve'. While Penny – a painter and a sculptor, someone accustomed to heavy lifting – cleared the land and made the ruin habitable (it had no running water, or electricity), Muriel found the quiet and the distance from clamorous friends and time-consuming bores conducive to writing. She knew that she had been accepted as part of the local community when, after some thirty years in residence, the priest asked her to say a few words to the congregation at Easter. Whenever she mentioned this, I had the impression that it afforded her as much pleasure as she took from any plaudit for her work.

Informed that we were carless, indeed that neither my wife nor I were in possession of a driving licence, Penny had immediately volunteered to pick us up at the Hotel Continentale. She and Muriel, it transpired, had delayed their departure to a more bearable clime to allow us to find our feet. As she drove, Penny pointed out landmarks, few of which we would be able to visit without access to our own transport. In recognition of this, Muriel and she had acquired two bikes from a shop in Arezzo. 'It's near the station,' she said, 'near to the tailor – Donati's – that Muriel recommended you to go to buy trousers. The bikes' tyres are a bit splitty so you may need to renew them. Also, I'm not sure if the brakes are working as they should. Best perhaps to test them before you go for a ride.'

It took about half an hour to reach San Giovanni. Penny drove the Alfa Romeo, which she handled as dexterously as if it were a dodgem car. Once off the main road we followed single-track roads which rose steeply and skirted the tiny, lemon-shaped village of Oliveto. All around were fields with straight rows of vines and wave upon wave of olive groves. Scattered among them were a few *contadini*, male and female farm workers, clearing overgrowth, scything grass or pruning purposefully. At a fork in the road we veered even more steeply and there, through the trees, stood San Giovanni.

It looked almost exactly as it did in Penny's sketch, with its low grey metal gate, red shutters, and semi-detached, deconsecrated church. The house, parts of which may date to the fifteenth century, was formerly occupied by a succession of priests not all of whom took their vow of celibacy seriously. One of the more libidinous fathers had added rooms as and when necessary to accommodate his growing flock. During the Second World War, the then occupant owned a radio that was tuned to the BBC and around which his parishioners would gather to hear the latest news. The whole area, remarked Penny, was under German occupation, and the inhabitants of Civitella suffered grievously from reprisals after two Nazis were killed by partisans. On the morning of 29 June 1944, inhabitants of the village awoke to the sound of doors being kicked in. Some were murdered in their beds while others were herded into the piazza and shot in groups of five. Many houses were set on fire and their occupants burned alive. No one was spared the wrath of the occupying force. The youngest to die was no more than one year old, the oldest eighty-four. In all, 244 people were massacred by the Hermann Göring Division before the village was liberated by the Black Watch, their arrival heralded by the sound of bagpipes from the *strada bianca*. In Oliveto, moreover, in what later became a school, there was a small concentration camp where Jews were held before their dispatch to Auschwitz. Penelope and Muriel's neighbour, Adolfo, told them that he had seen women being herded into trucks and butted in the backside by the rifle-wielding Germans. Long before Muriel was aware of the building's awful history, Penny added, she said that whenever she passed it she felt a shudder of horror.

As we got out of the car, Muriel, dressed in an elegant trouser suit, emerged from a gnarled door, beaming broadly and greeting the children as if she'd known them all their lives. She had in her hands two notebooks, one of which she presented to each of the children. Jennifer's was called 'Confidential' while Michael's was 'Underground'. 'Hide them from the Customs officials,' Muriel whispered. In 'Underground', on the first page, in distinctive cursive, Muriel had made a start on a diary, dated 20 October 1981: 'In Penelope's bedroom from a tiny hole in the ceiling descends a long white tube which coils on the floor, quivering. Vasco Nocciolini the plumber is arranging everything. Penelope wishes she had a camera. She says it is very interesting.'

Penny led the way up the steep stone staircase to our accommodation: two double bedrooms, an airy, old-fashioned bathroom with a bath, an exercise bike that looked as if it had never been used, and a large, dark oak-beamed sitting-room down the middle of which was a tall, packed bookcase. All the floors were tiled, and the staircase which led from the front door to the kitchen was of a stone that wore its vintage in its polished treads. In the sitting room we unlocked a couple of shutters and light flooded in and the landscape of Piero della Francesca lay framed before us in a spectrum of greens. There was no time to unpack. Lunch was taken in the kitchen around a small table: roast beef, tomato, mozzarella, basil, olive oil, bread, red wine. 'Do have a whisky,' said Muriel, flourishing a bottle of Famous Grouse. I hope I had the willpower to decline.

Muriel seemed pleased to have an audience and regaled us with anecdotes about her father, Bertie Camberg, whom, she said, she remembered accompanying to the races at Musselburgh, my home town. Once, when she was flush with cash, she herself had owned a part-share in a racehorse. It was called Lifeboat, she said, and its previous owner had been the Queen.

The kitchen at San Giovanni, site of an invasion of ants

The Spark Syndicate, as it was called, had two other members, Alan Maclean, her editor at Macmillan, and Maurice Macmillan, a director of the company. They paid £2,315 for Lifeboat. Muriel was most impressed by the horse's lineage. It was sired, she said, by Doutelle, a variation of the name of one of the boats in which Bonnie Prince Charlie and his party escaped to Skye after the failed uprising of 1745. Its trainer was Fred Winter, who as a jockey had twice won the Grand National. There was never any possibility of anyone aboard Lifeboat emulating that feat. On one of the few occasions that Muriel was able to watch it run it unseated its jockey before the race got underway. 'Too expensive', was her verdict on the sorry episode.

She had the air of someone who was demob happy. She and Penny were heading north, she said, in search of a breath of cooler air, though exactly where to was unspecified. They liked to just jump into the car and see where the road took them. All of Europe was open to them. Muriel was the happy passenger; Penny, who had a phobia about flying, was the driver. Sometimes, said Penny, when they were still en route, Muriel would open the glove compartment and help herself to a tot of whisky or brandy from one of the miniature bottles she kept in case of emergencies.

In the meantime, Penny volunteered to drive Rene and me to a nearby supermarket to stock up. 'The children will be all right with me,' said Muriel. 'Just call out "Muriel" if you want anything,' she told Michael and Jennifer. When we reached the supermarket it was closed, as most of Italy often is between the hours of one and four in the afternoon. To kill time Penny took us on a tour of haunts purportedly controlled by the Mafia, the aforementioned disco and the halt at Badia al Pino, at which trains stopped with unfathomable irregularity. At four on the dot the supermarket opened and we piled a trolley high, keenly aware that this would be the only such trip we could make. I tried to think of meals and what would be required to make them. There was no need to worry about wine and olive oil, said Penny, because they had plenty of their own. Usually, she did the harvesting of the olives, roping in any friends who happened to be around at the time. She then took them to the mill where they were pressed into oil. When she moved into San Giovanni a man she didn't know picked the olives, claiming that he had pruned and fertilised them. Penny agreed to share the crop and only later discovered that he had kept most of it.

We returned to San Giovanni around five when at last the temperature was falling and shadows were spreading across the garden. There was an abundance of apricots and quinces, peaches, plums and figs, all oozing beads of ripeness. Herbs, too, grew in profusion: rosemary, basil, mint, and many others I was unable to identify. The only interruption of the silence was a bird, invisible in the dense undergrowth, that sounded as if it was tapping out a telegraph message. Lizards clung to the walls of the house like untethered climbers to a cliff face. White butterflies, flocks of moths and fat bees flitted from flower to flower as if spoiled for choice on what to feast.

There had been a drama while we had been gone. As Jennifer played with the cats Michael had explored the grounds in which was a deep, dry well. Curious, he had lowered himself in and had been unable to clamber out. Jennifer fetched a branch that had broken off from a tree and with it attempted to pull him free but it was not long enough to reach him. She noticed that there was a black snake, no bigger than a hand, near her brother, which she thought it better not to mention. Meanwhile, one by one, the cats gathered to see what all the fuss was about. Jennifer decided that it was time to call for help and ran into the house shouting 'Muriel! Muriel!' as she had been instructed. Muriel emerged from her study and immediately took charge of the situation, calmly telling Michael that all he need do was climb out the way he had climbed in, which instructions he followed to the letter. Muriel was much amused by the incident which, over the years, she remembered and embellished, as she might one of her own macabrely comic stories, sometimes imagining what would have happened if she had tried to pull Michael out and he through his superior strength had inadvertently pulled her in.

A day or so later our hosts departed, leaving a series of notes for our attention. One, from Penelope, read: 'Please when answering the telephone don't say where we are to be reached. You don't know anything about either of us or our movements . . . You can't take messages! Especially you have never heard of Muriel Spark. We'd both be awfully grateful.' Should we have any problems Penny said it was best to contact Patrizia, the daily help, who would know what to do. Regarding the dogs we could always call the vet or the woman from whom they been obtained. She had a farm of sorts, whose livestock included a sheep that had 'married' a turkey. The mind boggled. Franco, Patrizia's handyman husband, could take care of anything to do with the 'bombola', the gas cylinder for the cooking stove. Penny and Muriel would call from time to time to see if everything was all right.

She had a couple of further warnings. One was about forest fires, which were common occurrences. The field opposite the house had burnt the previous year after someone in a passing car had thrown away a cigarette. The other concerned snakes, of which there were apparently many, among them vipers. 'The serum is in the refrigerator and the kit above . . .' On the plus side, there was a surfeit of plums falling from a tree down by the garage. 'Do eat them before anyone else does!' begged Penny.

Muriel's contribution was what she described as her 'foolproof' method of caging Mungo and Algie. First, she recommended, we should let the dogs out for their evening run. Then, half an hour before 'you seriously need to have them caged', we should take their food out to their pen and call them, whereupon 'Algernon will probably run in and Mungo won't'. We were not to worry about this. At this point in the proceedings Muriel advised giving Mungo a couple of minutes to make up his mind which, chances were, he would not. 'Then, if he is still not in, call Algie *out* of his cage, lock it with the food inside, and go back indoors for twenty minutes.' This, guaranteed Muriel, would do the trick. 'On return, you will find a very anxious Mungo only too eager to rush into the cage as soon as you unlock it.'

The manner in which Muriel wrote about the animals was indicative of her attitude towards them. They were emphatically not pets, and anyone who described them as such could expect a flea in their ear. They were animals that had become domesticated. Dogs were dogs and cats were cats and there the matter ended. She gave them names that seemed the most appealing and appropriate to her. Usually she and Penny acquired a cat or dog through friends or found them abandoned, a common practice in Italy where hunters had no compunction in killing anything that interfered with the pursuit of their sport. Over the years, Muriel said, she had lost several cats and dogs through poisoning. No one was ever caught. Indeed, to protest against this 'evil' as Muriel called it was to invite more such acts. 'With sickening regularity', she said of the huntsmen, 'they succeed in their aim.'

Not being someone particularly attached to animals, I didn't really take in all that was involved in looking after Mungo and Algie. They were big, powerful beasts and on first acquaintance they seemed only slightly less terrifying than the wolves to which they were related. They had large teeth which, when bared, looked more like tusks. Their bark was loud and fearsome, especially in the wee small hours when all it took to set them off was a rustle of a passing porcupine or a breath of wind in the grass. This was the signal for any other dogs in the vicinity to add their discordant contribution to the chorus. Once started the pandemonium could go on for hours; it was as if all the dogs in the Val di Chiana were known to one another and were having a frank exchange of views on matters of canine import. It felt as if we were sleeping in a kennel. Eventually, we resorted to throwing pails of precious water over the insomniac beasts which put a temporary stop to the commotion. Muriel wrote a lovely poem, 'Mungo Bays the Moon', inspired by Mungo's howling: 'He comes out of his kennel to sing / in the night, / My Mungo, my brown dog.'

It was a moot point who took whom for a walk, a duty we were required to perform at least once a day. Both Mungo and Algie strained so hard at the leash that whoever was supposed to be in charge of them found themselves being dragged in whichever direction they felt like taking. They had the strength and single-mindedness of huskies. How, I wondered, did Muriel manage to cope? But that was a daft question for I doubt she had ever tried. When on their evening run they would hurtle out of their cage like greyhounds released from the trap and rove over the countryside to the undoubted alarm of anyone in the vicinity who saw them approaching. Nowhere was out of bounds and they would leap like deer over the drystone walls, pad up and down the *strada bianca* as if they owned it and pursue unsuspecting cyclists toiling up the incline. On top of it all, they had the embarrassing habit of jumping up on strangers, salivating over their clothes and smothering them with unwanted affection. On one never-to-be forgotten occasion, Penny said, they had thrown themselves on a group of strolling nuns because under their habits they were wearing cast-off designer dresses that Muriel had given to them as presents.

Co-existing more or less harmoniously with Mungo and Algie were the 'some' outside cats which Penny had mentioned in her original letter. In fact, there were seven cats and few if any of them spent all of the time outdoors. Most treated the house like students, coming and going as they pleased, dropping by whenever they felt peckish, lounging around for a few hours, then disappearing no one knew where. One, called Baby Davie, was adopted by Jennifer. The others were Lucy, Frankie, Aurora, One-Eyed Riley, Little Grey and Miss Fisher. Muriel was more catlike than doglike. Her approach to novel-writing was to wait like a cat until she was ready to start and then, when she was satisfied that she done all the necessary research and thinking, she would 'pounce'. She once wrote that she envied cats' ability to purr, which she took as a sign of supreme contentment. In an *Encyclopaedia Britannica*, of which she had several well-thumbed editions, she had read that purring may indicate pleasure or pain. This she found surprising. 'I don't remember any time when a cat of mine purred in pain. I wonder if other cat owners have had such an experience.'

One day, as I was preparing lunch, I opened a shutter and watched in horror as the top of the cooker was covered instantly by a colony of tens of thousands of ants. One minute there was none, the next there was a black, swarming host. As I attempted desperately to brush them off, more and more ants arrived on the scene. There was no holding them back. While a bolognaise sauce bubbled on the stove, the ants massed around the pot as if laying siege to it. In the midst of this mayhem, One-Eyed Riley decided to get involved in the action and from the table he leapt like a trapeze artist on to my back, locking his claws into my bare shoulder before scraping his way down my back. My cries brought Rene rushing to the rescue. She immediately closed the shutter, which was the cue for the ants to retreat as fast as they had arrived.

With the departure of Muriel and Penelope we fell into a languorous routine. The days began at an hour at which we would normally have been asleep. Around six a.m. the first few *contadini* could be seen in the fields labouring away to a soundtrack of cocks crowing and the clicking of crickets. You could feel the heat rising as the sun emerged and the dew was burned off. A shimmering haze lay across the valley, adding to the feeling that you were living in another reality, above the cloud line, above reality itself, sharpening the senses, 'until' – as Muriel's friend Harold Acton observed about his own estate in the hills above Florence – 'the bats came squeaking into the dusk like the shrivelled souls of witches who had lost their broomsticks'.

One morning, before eight, Muriel rang to ask how we were doing. She was somewhere in France, a place whose name I didn't catch. The line was bad and I could only make out the odd phrase. It made me think of the anonymous

A few of the box files in which Muriel's voluminous archive was stored

caller in *Memento Mori* whose refrain is 'Remember you must die.' In a heat-induced stupor I began to doubt whether it was actually Muriel who had phoned or someone pretending to be her. Occasionally a tractor ground up the hill past the house, dust billowing in its wake. Around eleven the postman called, wished us '*buon giorno*', smiled and handed over the mail: letters and cards from Greenland, the United States, Oxford University, gifts (a video from Scotland), and Italian magazines wrapped in Cellophane with semi-naked girls on the cover. Now and then Adolfo dropped by, bearing a basket of vegetables and some eggs, which he would leave on the doorstep.

Late one morning half a dozen men and women on horseback appeared in the courtyard and asked with extravagant politeness if they could have some water. They had been out riding and sweat gleamed on their foreheads. It made me thirsty just to look at them and I hurried off to fetch glasses and a carafe. When I returned I realised I had a committed a *faux pas*; from their looks of amused bemusement I intuited that it was not the riders who needed water but their horses. By midday it was too hot to move a muscle. Nothing went by on the road; everyone was indoors for lunch. The afternoon was a time to doze and read. Muriel had selected a small pile of books she thought might be of interest to me. On top was Hilary Spurling's life of Paul Scott, author of *The Raj Quartet*. At one time Scott had been Muriel's agent. Tucked inside Spurling's biography was a clipping of the *Times Literary Supplement*'s review, in the margin of which had been scribbled: 'Shouldn't have thought he was worth a biography.' Years later Scott's name came up in conversation. Muriel said: 'There was a period when I used to see him quite often and dined at his house with, oddly, his wife hovering in another room, not joining us at the table.' 'He was after you,' said Penny. Muriel nodded. Scott was not the only man whose unwelcome attentions she had had to fend off in the 1950s in London.

Among the other books she gave me were *Family and Friends* by Anita Brookner, *The Oxford Book of Friendship*, *Learning to Look* – the autobiography of John Pope-Hennessy, and Betty T. Bennett's *Mary Diana Dods: A Gentleman and a Scholar*. Muriel had come across the last-mentioned while researching her own book on Mary Shelley. Dods was the illegitimate daughter of a Scottish landowner who assumed the identity of two men, one of whom was Walter Sholto Douglas. Thereafter she – or perhaps he – had eloped abroad with a friend of Mary's called Isabella Robinson. Once, said Muriel, she had travelled to San Terenzo, near Lerici in the Golfo dei Poeti, to visit the Shelleys' last house. She hadn't expected to see inside but its owner, an Italian doctor, offered to show her round. It was much as it was in the 1820s, including the terrace – 'the location of so many of those young people's psychic crises and infectious hysteria' – from which Mary watched and waited in vain for the boat carrying her husband Percy to return.

One day, having run perilously low on essential provisions, in particular ice-cream, Jennifer and I decided to cycle to Civitella. It was uphill all the way. On a previous occasion she and Michael had planned to walk there. Each had their own water bottle, walking stick, Mars bars, pencils and paper, and the 3,000 lira map of the area I'd bought at the station bookstall in Arezzo. They reckoned they would reach Civitella in around an hour or so, gorge on ice-cream and Coca-Cola, and return in time for supper, all the while never having been missed by Rene and me. The plan was scuppered when Michael picked up a nasty infection in his foot, which swelled alarmingly and required professional medical attention. On our cycling trip the temperature was in the nineties so Jennifer and I walked most of the way. Or at least I did. Jennifer sat on the bike's saddle while I wheeled it up the rutted road, dripping sweat, cursing my foolhardiness and muttering about mad dogs and Scotchmen going out in the midday sun. Fortunately, the *alimentari*, the grocer's shop-cum-bar, in Civitella was open. A few wizened locals were inside in the gloom, sheltering from the glare, sipping white wine and playing cards. When I explained in pidgin Italian that we had cycled from Oliveto, they looked at me as if I was deranged.

Jennifer and I took our drinks outside and sat on the town walls from where we had a panoramic view of the valley and far beyond. There was not a breath of wind and you could hear in the distance the faint rumble of traffic. We bought several litres of ice-cream and then leapt on the bike and were soon hurtling downhill at a speed which the brakes were unable to reduce significantly. Jennifer, oblivious to any danger, urged me to go faster but we couldn't go any faster than we were going. At any moment I expected to pitch into a ditch or crash into a tree. In little over five minutes we were home, me white with fear, Jennifer puce as a plum, the bike coated in dust, the ice-cream still more or less frozen.

On another day we returned from a walk to find the kitchen floor awash. It wasn't raining and we could find no other source for the pool that was deepening by the minute. Armed with an Italian phrasebook, Rene raced to our nearest neighbour, a *contadino*, who arrived with a couple of friends, none of whom seemed to know how to solve what was becoming a parlous situation. Eventually, a plumber was summoned and he quickly realised that instead of turning off the electricity as we had been instructed to do whenever we left the house we had switched on a water pump. The walls soon dried out but the water left an unsightly mark which I covered up with whitewash bought in nearby Monte San Savino. On our departure from San Giovanni I left a note telling Muriel and Penny of the drama and what I had done to make amends, which neither of them ever brought up.

Princes Street, Edinburgh, in the 1930s. The clock in the distance is always set a few minutes fast

pennant from Flodden Field, the scene in 1513 of a disastrous Scottish defeat at the hands of the English, still hangs limply and from whose pulpit John Knox railed against Mary, Queen of Scots – over George IV Bridge and down the widening gyre of Victoria Street, like the descent into the dankest of dungeons, to the Grassmarket, where in *The Prime of Miss Jean Brodie* the destitute and deprived gathered and a man 'just sat'. In Edinburgh, history is a living, indelible, inescapable reality. For Sandy Stranger, the sole member of a select group of girls – the crème de la crème – who will betray Miss Brodie, it is her 'first experience of a foreign country, which intimates itself by its new smells and shapes and its new poor'.

This was the impression it created on Muriel Camberg when she was growing up. Edinburgh, more so perhaps than other cities of a comparable size, is layered like an onion, in which members of one profession – lawyers, doctors, divines and dominies – can live for decades without getting to know those employed in others very well, or even at all. It is also a patchwork of distinctive, characterful villages, some immeasurably more prosperous than others, each with its defined borders. Moreover, it is a place in which where you live is a mark of the class to which you belong. This is manifested in the clothes people wear, the shops they frequent, the churches they favour and with whom they choose to socialise. The simplest way to register where someone stands on the social ladder is to enquire which school they attended; in contrast to other parts of Scotland, Edinburghers are more likely to have gone to a private school than a state one. Might this be why, as Muriel observed, they have 'a sense of civic superiority'? American friends of mine, invited to a dinner party in the New Town, were once asked to which school they sent their children. Immediately, they sensed a trap was being set but, having no offspring, felt they could safely parry the question. No such luck. 'But which school would you send your children to if you had any?' countered the host. Of course snobbery, of which Muriel was an acute and critical observer – see her short story 'The Snobs' – is the unspoken reason for such divisiveness. Her school, James Gillespie's, fictionalised in *The Prime of Miss Jean Brodie* as Marcia Blaine School, was one of a number in the city endowed by philanthropic merchants and burghers. But it was not one of the elite establishments, such as Edinburgh Academy, of which Robert Louis Stevenson was an alumnus, or the venerable Royal High School, at which Walter Scott did not – in his own estimation – make 'any great figure'. Gillespie's eponymous benefactor was a wealthy eighteenth-century snuff and tobacco merchant who had a shop in the Royal Mile, which later became an Italian restaurant much favoured by us night-hawks working at the *Scotsman* newspaper because of the generous hours kept by its proprietor. For Muriel, Gillespie – 'humbly born, a son of the people' – epitomised Edinburgh. His gift, it might be argued, was one of the factors that led to her becoming the writer she did. On her father's modest salary her parents could not afford the fees the school required, and they took in boarders to supplement Bernard's income. Only latterly, when Muriel's good grades led to her winning scholarships, did such financial headaches pass.

She spent twelve years at Gillespie's, every one of which she relished. As she later remarked, 'I was always happy at a desk.' When in 1997 she was awarded the David Cohen British Literature Prize for a 'lifetime's achievement' – she put her share of prize money (£30,000) towards 'a lovely, new, suitable, motor car', an Alfa Romeo. She was given an additional £10,000 to bestow on a cause close to her heart, and chose Gillespie's, specifying that it should be spent on the art department. There it was that she encountered moustachioed, Mussolini-loving Miss Christina Kay, the teacher on whom she doted and on whom she was loosely to model Miss Jean Brodie. Even as a schoolgirl, Muriel knew that in this idiosyncratic, inspirational teacher she had found a soulmate of sorts, someone special, who embraced the classroom as others do the stage, and whom she could transform into the kind of character that combined charm and charisma with the ability to brainwash the impressionable.

Muriel's class photo from James Gillespie's School in 1930. Muriel is second from the right in the third row from the front. The teacher, Miss Christina Kay, was the character on whom the fictional Miss Jean Brodie was based

Miss Kay was sufficiently different from other teachers to make Muriel appreciate that, were she so inclined, the effect she could have had on her young charges might have been calamitous. In effect, in her own domain, she was all powerful; what she said was taken as gospel. As Muriel recalled in her autobiography, *Curriculum Vitae*, it was Miss Kay who foresaw that she would become a writer – 'I hardly had a choice in the matter.' Miss Kay took Muriel and Muriel's lifelong friend Frances Niven to plays and lectures, concerts, galleries and museums, conspiratorially imploring them not to tell their schoolmates lest she be accused of favouritism by them, or of inappropriate behaviour by her superiors. She liked to personalise her lessons, which, if not specifically discouraged by the inflexible rules of the educational authorities, would certainly have been frowned upon. On one occasion, Muriel recalled, Miss Kay interrupted a lesson to tell how she had gone to the gas office to query a bill. 'Our class of girls, incipient feminists, was totally enthralled by Miss Kay's account of how the clerks tittered and nudged each other: a *female* desiring to discuss the details of a gas bill! "But", said Miss Kay, "I went through that bill with the clerk point by point. He at first said he couldn't see any mistake. But when I asked to see the manager he had another look at the bill. He consulted with one of his colleagues. Finally, he came to me with a very long face. He admitted there had been an error in calculation. I made them amend the bill, and I paid it there and then. *That*", said Miss Kay, with her sweet, wise smile, "taught them to sneer at a businesslike young woman".'

It was while she was at Gillespie's, 'at some public Scott-centenary celebration', that Muriel was crowned – literally crowned – Queen of Poetry. If that sounds unlikely, it is only a sign of how things have changed in the intervening years. The most influential and visible literary figure in that era was Christopher Murray Grieve, who wrote under the name of Hugh MacDiarmid. Born in 1892 in the Border town of Langholm, he went to school in Edinburgh. His first collection of poems, *Sangshaw*, appeared in 1925, which was followed a year later by *Penny Wheep*. Both are remarkable for their lyrical beauty and exquisite use of Lallans, an artificial or 'synthetic' form of the Scots dialect of which MacDiarmid was the major practitioner. Also in 1926 he published his masterpiece, 'A Drunk Man Looks at the Thistle', a poem of 2,685 lines fizzing with ideas and pyrotechnic flourishes which at a stroke catapulted the literature of his native heath into the twentieth century.

A communist and a nationalist, MacDiarmid, whose *cri de guerre* was always to be 'whaur extremes meet', was a gifted and inveterate polemicist who delighted in overturning apple carts and pulverising received opinions. 'The poetry I want,' he wrote, 'turns its back contemptuously on all the cowardly and brainless staples of Anglo-Scottish literature – the whole base business of people who do not act but are merely acted upon – people whose "unexamined lives" are indeed "not worth having", though they include every irresponsible who occupies a "responsible position" in Scotland today, practically all our Professors, all our M.P.s, and certainly all our "Divines", all our peers and great landlords and big business men, the teaching profession almost without exception, almost all our writers – "half glow-worms and half newts".'

If as a young girl Muriel knew of MacDiarmid and his impact on contemporary Scottish literature she never alluded to it. The poetry she read then was of an earlier period. I am not even sure that as an adult she read his work. This may be explained by her estrangement from Scotland. It must be said that she was not sympathetic to MacDiarmid's politics or, indeed, the idiom in which he wrote. She felt that writing in a language which only relatively few people could read was counter-productive. English, not Scots, was the language in which she felt most comfortable. 'I see no point', she once wrote, 'in a dialect that the average intelligent reader in Essex or Worcestershire cannot understand. I see no point in offering Scots dialects (which in any case are not regionally constant) to the intelligent readers in the United States or in Australia. The object of art is to diffuse intellectual pleasure . . .' This would have baffled MacDiarmid. But where she and he would have agreed was that poetry was the highest of the literary forms. It was one to which she aspired to write. If, as she averred, she always had difficulty in seeing herself as a novelist, the same could not be said of her as a poet.

In the National Library of Scotland is a rare, paper-bound copy of a little book, *The Door of Youth*, published in 1930. Subtitled 'Poems From Edinburgh School Magazines', it has a preface by John Buchan, one of the most popular writers of the time. Muriel, then age twelve, is represented by five poems, more than any of the other contributors, by far the majority of whom were several years older than she was. The book opens with 'To Everybody' in which she asserts her affinity with poetry. While the artist has his canvas, the dreamer his dreams and the scholar his books, what she loves best, and into which she puts her 'zeal and zest', is verse.

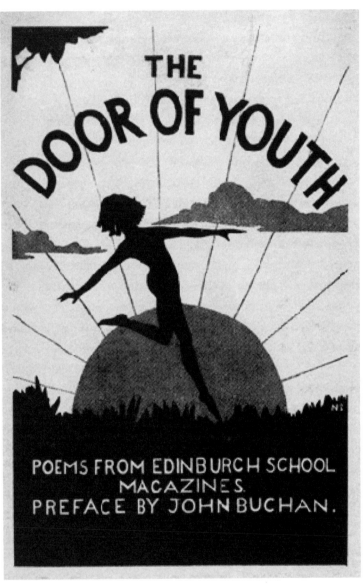

The Door of Youth booklet, published in 1930, in which five of Muriel's childhood poems appeared

Another of her poems is 'The Winding of the Horn'. Obviously influenced by the Border ballads, many of which she knew off by heart, she bemoans in it the hunting of a deer. Yet another poem is called 'Time':

Time, Time, what is Time?
　　Which brings to end our pleasure?
　Oh, in those glorious realms beyond
　　　There are no things of measure.

Such technical assurance and grasp of rhythm is impressive. Three years later, aged fifteen, she won a competition held among pupils from Edinburgh schools to commemorate the one hundredth anniversary of the death of Sir Walter Scott. Her poem, 'Out of a Book', was printed as a broadsheet, copies of which were sold for a penny. The proceeds went to the Children's Shelter in the High Street.

Not far from the family home in Bruntsfield was Morningside Public Library. Its staff used proudly to boast it was the busiest of its kind in Britain, and so it often seemed. Muriel made the short trip two or three times a week, in the early evening as the light began to fail or on a Saturday morning when queues would form outside its doors before it opened, in the hope of being the first to borrow the latest additions to the collection or to request titles approvingly reviewed in the Saturday edition of the *Scotsman*. Once, in the 1970s, during a local government strike, it fell to me as a young librarian – and trade union activist – to picket Morningside library and explain to patrons the nobility of our cause, the gist of which I cannot now recall. It was a brutally cold day and as I and my fellow comrades waved our banners, chanted slogans and stamped our feet to keep frostbite at bay a chauffeur-driven limousine pulled up at the kerbside. Out stepped a woman of a certain age swathed in fur and burdened with a pile of books which she handed over to me, as you might a used cup and saucer to a butler. I tried to explain who I was and what was going on but the woman was unimpressed. 'What on earth are you talking about?' she said. 'A strike? In the library? Don't be ridiculous!' She pushed past me and made for the entrance only to discover it locked, whereupon, muttering darkly, she got back in the car. When I told Muriel the story she laughed and nodded appreciatively. In her youth, she said, she had witnessed many such incidents, not least after she had left school and was working in Small's department store in Princes Street. What seemed to amuse her most, though, was the thought of me manning the barricades outside a library.

Muriel in 1957, the year in which *The Comforters*, her first novel, was published

A voracious reader, Muriel was in the habit of taking the library tickets of her mother, father and brother, allowing her to borrow more books than she was able to carry. As she recalled, 'My after-school life was divided between lending libraries and the corner of the kitchen where I curled up with my loot.' In a real sense the library was her university. Now and then Muriel would mention that she had not gone to university, and sometimes I detected a note of regret in her voice. What, potentially, had she missed? Would she have made the grade in academia? On the other hand, had she gone to university, she would not have been able to read whatever she wanted without interference. Her reading was unprogrammed, serendipitous. I imagine her wandering up and down the ranks of books in Morningside, each one meticulously filed, spines placed flush with the shelf, fiction arranged alphabetically, non-fiction classified in accordance with the same system as used by the Library of Congress in Washington DC. Here were worlds beyond Edinburgh: exotic, exciting, imaginary, fantastical, a mere stroll away from the modest flat in which she lived.

Poetry was what she read mainly. John Masefield, whom Miss Kay took her to hear recite his work and whom in later life she was to meet, was an early favourite, especially his narrative verse. She read as she would never read again – 'for I was destined to poetry by all my mentors'. Wordsworth, Browning, Tennyson and Swinburne were followed by the Georgians: Edmund Blunden, Rupert Brooke, Walter de la Mare, W. B. Yeats, Robert Bridges and Alice Meynell, 'the only woman among them'. Conspicuous by its absence is any mention of Scottish poets. Of course she knew Scott and his *Minstrelsy of the Scottish Border*, Burns ('so "modern" a genius, so uninhibited, full of virility, a hard drinker, bawdy, garrulous, at times self-

his blue Tardis at the bottom of Victoria Street. It was an edgy quarter even in daylight. Come nightfall, however, it grew more aggressive and regressive. One of its many pubs is called The Last Drop in recognition of the fact that the Grassmarket was where public hangings took place. Its sign is a gibbet.

Edinburgh then was a dark and sooty and odiferous place. It had long rejoiced in the nickname 'Auld Reekie' on account of the coal smoke that poured into the atmosphere and blackened the buildings, and the noxious smells that were a result of the insanitary habits of the citizenry. Robert Chambers, in his *Traditions of Edinburgh*, traced the origin of the phrase to the tale, probably apocryphal, of an old gentleman in Fife, Durham of Largo, who in the mid-seventeenth century, was in the habit of regulating the time of evening worship by the appearance of smoke on the other side of the Firth of Forth. As the smoke increased in density, a sure sign that Edinburghers were preparing their supper, he would call the family into the house, saying: 'It's time now, bairns, to tak' the beuks, and gang to our beds, for yonder's Auld Reekie, I see, putting on her nicht-cap!' Things had improved by Muriel's day but even then there was a distinct flavour to Edinburgh. Near where she lived was McEwan's brewery at Fountainbridge which added a sickly-sweet, yeasty tang to the air. At night, there was little in the way of illumination and you often heard someone approach before you saw them. It seemed an ideal place for intrigue and debauchery.

Among Muriel's near contemporaries was David Daiches, whose father, Rabbi Dr Salis Daiches, was the leader of the local Jewish community. David was born in 1912 in Sunderland, and moved north with his family a few years later. How well he knew Muriel has been a matter of some dispute. In seeking background information for my original interview with her in 1990 I contacted David. He told me he had been acquainted with Muriel – whom he knew as Minnie – as a young girl, and that her parents had been married in Edinburgh by his father. I didn't question this, though perhaps I ought to have done; after all, Muriel was six years younger than David, a significant gap at that stage in life. Ever a stickler for accuracy, Muriel wrote to put me right, saying that her parents were not married by Rabbi Daiches – which would have been impossible, given that he only took up his position eight years after they were married in London in 1911 – and that she had never been known as Minnie. 'I have always been called Muriel.'

As storms in teacups go this may seem a minor one but the fuss it caused may be read as indicative of attitudes to Muriel in some Edinburgh circles. It even reached the pages of the *Times Literary Supplement* and from time to time thereafter it would flare up again, confirming Muriel's opinion of 'well-meaning scholars' who are destined to regurgitate the false statements of their peers. As she put it: 'Lies are like fleas hopping from here to there, sucking the blood of the intellect.' Quite recently, Owen Dudley Edwards, a well-known Edinburgh academic, accused her of squirting 'vitriol' at David Daiches (who died in 2005), and of 'mendacity', which would have seen him facing a libel charge had he said so in print when she was alive. Edwards also suggested that Muriel's childhood poetry was inspired by David's, though he offered no evidence to show that she had ever read it, which is not surprising given that Daiches's work appeared in his own school's magazine – George Watson's – which Muriel would not in normal circumstances have had access to.

In his delightful memoir, *Two Worlds*, first published in 1957, David makes no mention of Muriel, which would only be curious had he known her as well as he said he did. The book's title refers to his Jewish heritage and the constricted society in which he was brought up, and the pull of Scotland at large, from which David and his elder brother Lionel, a colourful advocate, had been kept apart for much of their childhood. The Daicheses, David reflected, did not live between two worlds but were part of both: integration and assimilation were seen as natural and desirable. 'The Edinburgh Jewish community was small – about four hundred families,' he wrote. 'Though I knew the other Jewish children in the city, and regularly attended their parties in the winter party season, I was intimate with none. In some respects I felt more cut off from them than from my Presbyterian classmates and street companions.' One might think that had David known someone like Muriel, he would have thought it worth mentioning.

Muriel, for her part, in *Curriculum Vitae*, makes no mention of David or Lionel or their father or, indeed, visits to the synagogue in nearby Graham Street, which she surely would have done had it been a regular occurrence. Some writers, including Edwards, have seen this omission as a 'repudiation' or wilful abandonment of her Jewish heritage, which it most surely was not. Muriel was unashamed of her history and antecedents and never made any attempt to hide her Jewishness. It was part of who she was. But it was not all of who she was. Her father was Jewish but he was not insistently so; her mother was brought up as a Christian, most likely agreeing to be married in a synagogue to suit her husband. Jewishness, as Muriel would say until she was blue in the face, comes through the maternal line; thus she was not in the strictest sense a Jew, though, she added, such nuances would have counted for little to the Nazis. As she noted: 'I find it impossible to separate the Jewess within myself from the Gentile, even for the sake of argument. The attempt is absurd in any case if the two strains exist uncomplainingly amongst one's own bones.' But try as she might to put the argument to bed it had, as we shall see, a tendency to waken in the night and bawl for all its worth, causing pain and grief to those on both sides of it.

At first, on that visit to Edinburgh in 1962 to be at her father's bedside, Muriel had stayed with her mother and her son, Robin, in the flat overlooking Bruntsfield links in which she was born and had been brought up. But it was not an arrangement that suited her. Robin was moody and insisted she leave, while her mother, Cissy, was drinking 'more than was good for her' – as they say hereabouts – and in her cups doubtless saying unpleasant things. The flat was in need of a good scrub, which Muriel – though rarely domestically inclined, not least because as a young girl her mother absolved her of any such responsibility – gave it. Having said that, she always had a preference for hotels where life's irritating necessities were taken care of and she could devote herself to the business of writing.

Her fondness for her father was evident whenever she spoke of him. Photographs suggest he was a dapper fellow, his tie militarily knotted, his suit looking as if had been recently dry-cleaned, not a hair out of place. He was an engineer, and had a marked Edinburgh accent. Unlike the two elder Camberg children, who had come with their parents from Lithuania, he was born in Scotland. 'He wore the same sort of clothes as the other fathers and spoke as they did,' Muriel recalled. 'So he was no problem.' Bertie was a keen racegoer and a backer of horses and on occasion took Muriel to Musselburgh race course. I told Muriel that it was at the race course that I used to play football on a pitch in the lee of a gasworks, its noxious fumes spewing forth unchecked. Muriel couldn't place it but remembered that there was a golf course – the first to host the Open Championship – around which the horses ran, and that Oliver Cromwell and his army of Roundheads had camped there before and after the Battle of Dunbar. Like me, Muriel had learned from an early age the rhyme which is repeated in *The Prime of Miss Jean Brodie*:

Edinburgh, Leith,
Portobello, Musselburgh
And Dalkeith.

When her father died, Muriel wrote a short essay in which she recalled those few limbo-like weeks. 'What Images Return' was commissioned by Karl Miller when he was literary editor of the *New Statesman* and republished by him in a book, *Memoirs of Modern Scotland*, in celebration of Hector MacIver, an influential and inspirational teacher who had taught Miller at Edinburgh's Royal High School. The essay is about Scotland, Edinburgh and Muriel herself. The defining word is 'nevertheless' which, she speculated, may be used more often in Edinburgh than anywhere else.

'I can see the lips of tough elderly women in musquash coats taking tea at MacVittie's, enunciating this word of final justification, I can see the exact gesture of head and chin and gleam of eye that accompanied it. The sound was roughly "nivethelace" and the emphasis was a heartfelt one. I believe myself to be fairly indoctrinated by the habit of thought which calls for this word. In fact I approve of the ceremonious accumulation of weather forecasts and barometer-readings that pronounce for a fine day, before letting rip on the statement: "Nevertheless, it's raining." I find that much of my literary composition is based on the nevertheless idea. I act upon it. It was on the nevertheless principle that I turned Catholic.'

In a sense 'What Images Return' was Muriel's valedictory salute to her homeland. Written nearly a quarter of a century after she actually had left, it is her rationale of why she had become what she termed 'a constitutional exile'. As Penny is at pains to explain, Muriel did not actually consider herself an exile, suggestive as that is of banishment and enforced separation. It is true that her absence was long and that her visits – usually to see her mother and son – were infrequent over the years, not least because of the possibility of unpleasantness on the part of her son and her ex-husband, whom she was always anxious might turn up at public gatherings and make a scene. The assumption grew that she had turned her back on Scotland and that she felt she had outgrown it. There is more than a degree of truth in that although she did consider moving back when life in Rome was becoming increasingly chaotic and dangerous. For Muriel, however, Scotland was too small, too inward-looking, too mindful of other people's business, too mean-spirited, too unreceptive to the wider world. As the novelist Allan Massie, one of Muriel's earliest and most loyal champions, observed: 'Pride in the Scot who had gone forth and prospered was permitted: as long as you remembered he would have been a bloody fool to stay at home.'

Typical of this frame of mind was another novelist, Robin Jenkins. In an interview in 1999, in *Scotland*, a short-lived magazine, in which he was billed as 'Scotland's most senior, most distinguished novelist', he said he did not like Muriel's work – or for that matter Iris Murdoch's – because he did not understand their characters:

> They are the kind of people I would never meet, and never want to meet . . . Muriel Spark's *The Prime of Miss Jean Brodie* was set in Scotland. Mind you, she was brought up in Scotland, but then she left and never wrote about Scotland again. And you'll find it very difficult to get any real Scots person accepting her as a Scottish writer. I know the English do. They think she is a wonderful Scottish writer, on the strength of *Miss Jean Brodie*. But all the other novels, they're set in Venice, they're set in London, particularly, I just don't get it, I can't understand how I, as a Scottish writer, could be content to stay in London, and write about the English. Never! Never! And I don't know if there were any really good Scottish novels ever written by anybody in those circumstances.

Jenkins's view is symptomatic of a problem endemic in Scotland in the not so distant past. He was by no means alone in holding views such as these. Certain Scots have always resented those who leave for whatever reason. It makes them feel betrayed, belittled, abandoned, and the opportunity to bring down to size anyone who had succeeded abroad and found fame and fortune would always be seized. There's a saying that sums this up: I kent your faither. It means I know who you are, I know where you come from, how dare you get above yourself, you're no better than me. For her part Muriel would have had the perfect riposte: 'Who is this Robin Jenkins? What gives him the right to talk about me like that? I've never heard of him.'

The soot-smeared, wardrobe-sized hearth in the kitchen at San Giovanni

3
ALTOGETHER A EUROPEAN

*You may have heard of Samuel Cramer, half poet, half journalist,
who had to do with a dancer called the Fanfarlo. But, as you
will see, it doesn't matter if you have not.*

'THE SERAPH AND THE ZAMBESI'

In 1951 Muriel entered, and won, a short story competition
which changed the course of her life. It was organised by
the *Observer* newspaper and attracted 6,700 entries, including
many from well-established writers tantalised by the thought
of the £250 prize money. Muriel was the successful one.
Though not far from the breadline, she bought herself a dress
and a complete set of Proust. It was the kind of thing she did
throughout her life whenever she had a windfall. She also gave
£50 to Derek Stanford, and sent a similar sum to her parents to
pay for her son's bar mitzvah. Money did not tend to linger long
in Muriel's bank account; when flush she would seldom pass a
beggar without handing over a few coins and she always tipped
generously, as much to cheer up herself as the lucky waiter or
cabbie. She knew what it was to be poor and it pained her to see
anyone reduced to panhandling.

Her winning story, which perplexed a few readers
and entranced many more, was called 'The Seraph and the
Zambesi'. 'It may interest you to know', Muriel later told me,
'that the entries . . . had to be anonymous. One signed with a
pseudonym and attached an envelope with the real name and
address inside. My pseudonym was "Aquarius".' The paper's

literary editor, Philip Toynbee, who was one of the judges, rang her with the good news. Initially, he said, he thought the story must have been written by a man. If Muriel was meant to take this as a compliment, she did not. In the notebook in which she kept a record of everything she sent for possible publication she simply wrote, 'Got it.' When the story appeared in the paper, its editor, David Astor, delivered a copy personally to her at her furnished rooms in London in the wee small hours, a courtesy she never forgot.

Her triumph was the talk of the town. Doris Lessing called it 'a prodigious debut . . . I remember reading it with the exhilaration that comes from the unexpected, from agreeable surprise'. Overnight, it transformed Muriel's fortunes, to such an extent that a year later she entered into a feisty correspondence with Her Majesty's Inspector of Taxes, who had noticed that she had not included the prize money in her list of earnings for the previous year. This, remarked the vigilant civil servant, should have been included as part of her 'professional earnings'. He added: 'I shall be glad if you will let me know for the purposes of my records how you have maintained yourself during the year.'

Muriel's response was typically prompt and business-like. It was her understanding, she wrote indignantly, that the amount she had received was exempt from taxation. It was, moreover, not £100, as the taxman had indicated, but £250. Were this to be included as part of her income, thus making her liable to pay tax, she sought the right to appeal. 'The prize was not, in any sense, professional earnings. Indeed there was considerable outcry when I was awarded the prize, that it had not gone to a professional short-story writer. There was an article in *The Bookseller* complaining bitterly of the fact. In *The Observer* of

30 Dec, 1951, it was clearly stated, in connection with this prize, that this was my first short story.'

'I am not a short-story writer,' she further insisted. 'I am a critic and biographer. I doubt I shall ever have another short story published. The only *creative* writing I do is poetry. I went in for the competition much as one might enter a crossword puzzle contest, and no-one was more surprised than myself when I won it. And, as I say, I had to put up with a great deal of criticism on the grounds that I was not a "professional short-story writer".'

The taxman was not persuaded by her protestations. 'You have been exercising the profession of a writer and looking at the matter financially it is hardly possible, I suggest, to draw a hard and fast line between one form of literary earnings and another. I shall be glad to hear that on reconsideration you agree.' There is nothing in Muriel's archive to indicate whether she or the taxman came out on top. What we do know is that this marked the end of one phase of her life and the beginning of another as the critic and biographer was eclipsed by the writer of fiction. For a while she continued to work on non-fiction books in 'partnership' with Derek Stanford, but it was evident that her ambition and inclination now lay elsewhere. 'The Seraph and the Zambesi' would not be her last short story.

Reading it some years later – with its suggestions of what later came to be tagged magical realism – and appreciating the transformative effect it had on her and her career, I thought it might be a good idea to institute a similar competition in *Scotland on Sunday*. Its editor, Andrew Jaspan, one of the few of his kind actually to be interested in books, immediately agreed and arranged a lunch with a potential sponsor. Under his own name Allan Shiach ran the Macallan malt whisky company.

Using the pseudonym Allan Scott he wrote and produced films such as *Don't Look Now* and *Castaway* in collaboration with Nicholas Roeg. Could there be a better partner? A deal was soon sealed over a vintage dram in Edinburgh's Cafe Royal and the Macallan / Scotland on Sunday short story competition was launched. As well as Allan and myself, the judges were the novelist William Boyd and Muriel. In a letter responding to my invitation, she wrote: 'The short story is an incomparable test of good writing. And I always welcome any tendency to make Scottish writing realise its own identity. It is at present generally judged by Home Counties' standards – a "regional" offshoot. Scottish culture in general seems to have become confined to folk-dancing.' How, she inquired, did we intend to define 'new writers and writing in Scotland'? She suggested we adopt the criterion 'Scottish by formation', which we gratefully did.

From the outset the prize, which was awarded annually for a number of years, attracted more than 2,000 entries. Among its winners were Michel Faber and Ali Smith, both of whose careers it helped fly. That first year it was won by Dilys Rose, who lived in a flat in Edinburgh just a few streets away from the one in which Muriel had been brought up. Rose's work, 'A Little Bit of Trust', she remarked, was an 'easy' winner. She liked its atmosphere, imagination and realism. Above all it was a story, 'sharp and unsentimental', which, now one comes to think of it, is not a bad description of Muriel herself.

In the story of Muriel's own life, Derek Stanford occupies the unenviable role of cad and betrayer. He was her Iago and her Mark Anthony. They first met in 1947 when she was working at the Poetry Society and he was looking for some kind of literary work. In *A Far Cry from Kensington* she reimagined him as Hector Bartlett, a pushy, third-rate hack – a *'pisseur de copie'* or 'urinator of journalistic copy' who 'vomited literary matter' – with upper-class pretensions. Whenever his name cropped up in conversation, which it did from time to time, it was invariably in the guise of someone whom she had once trusted, perhaps even loved, and whom she now thought of as beyond the pale. She was well aware that no matter what she said or did she could not erase him from her past.

It was largely because of Stanford that from the mid-1950s onwards Muriel kept virtually every scrap of paper that came into her possession. It was her protection against the lies and myths which, like toxic chemicals, seeping through the soil into the water supply, pollute everything they come into contact with. When they were close they would write to each other almost daily. In 1948, for example, after Muriel was sacked from the Poetry Society, it was Stanford who organised a poetry reading in her support and petitioned T. S. Eliot ('a subtle precise-minded Possum, master of the great conditional') and Graham Greene for money on her behalf when she collapsed after using the appetite suppressant Dexedrine. In *Curriculum Vitae*, she noted that her success so affected him that it induced a nervous breakdown.

Some years after their romance ended, a hard-up Stanford sold documents he had taken from Muriel without permission to two American universities. This was unforgivable. By this time, the early 1960s, she was a celebrity, the fêted author of *The Prime of Miss Jean Brodie*. A year after its appearance, Stanford compounded the offence by writing *Muriel Spark: A Biographical and Critical Study*, the first book on her. In it he described her as a combination of Mary, Queen of Scots – like the ill-fated monarch, Muriel was Catholic and had red hair – and Elizabeth I, which stretched the imagination somewhat. 'Surrounded by the young poets like Bess by her courtiers,' he wrote, 'she would sit perched on the side of the table, her short but sturdy legs dangling like those of a child who cannot reach the floor.' For Muriel, this truly was the limit. A line had been crossed and there could be no possibility of rapprochement. Unfazed, Stanford added to her ire when in 1977 he returned to the subject in *Inside the Forties*, a gossipy memoir in which Muriel was given a prominent part.

Here, the portrait he contrived managed to be simultaneously flattering and patronising, supportive and sexist. She was 'very much a feminine Shelley', he wrote, who 'lived solely for art' and who 'excelled at caricature, not copy'. He recalled how when Muriel was at the Poetry Society she found it necessary on occasion to repel the advances of male grandees who 'thought that their support of her and her programme should be repaid in favours'. One of these sex pests had plans to install her in the flat at the top of the Society's headquarters where – as Stanford put it – 'he would carnally possess her in every room'. Muriel was unreceptive to these crude overtures which, on one occasion, led to a struggle during which she lost a front tooth. In those days such boorish behaviour was accepted as rather the norm. Women like Muriel, irrespective of their marital status, were deemed fair game by predatory louts who expected to be rewarded simply for being allowed to join their company. Joan Wyndham, in her wartime diary, recalled how, on first encountering Dylan Thomas, he cadged a drink then smothered her in wet beery kisses, an experience which she likened to being embraced by an intoxicated octopus.

Muriel shopping at Peckham Rye market, 1961, the year in which *The Prime of Miss Jean Brodie* was published

'I tried to tell myself that I was being kissed by a great poet . . .'

It was Stanford's greed and disloyalty that most upset Muriel. No one knew better than him the importance she placed on the fidelity of friends. 'In her own private scale of values,' he wrote, 'loyalty to her own person stood first. About this, she was both tremendously susceptible and enormously demanding.' The books of his in which she features are replete with errors of fact and wild imaginative flights which have been repeated down the decades without challenge by countless other writers and scholars. In addition, Muriel sensed – rightly in my view – that Stanford was envious of her, as is wearisomely common in literary circles.

Such upsetting experiences could have made her feel wary of forging new acquaintances but that was not the case. Muriel was keen to meet new people and was always interested in them and their lives. Her letters were warm and solicitous and signed off 'Fond love'. She was preternaturally curious, as a writer must be, but she was also sympathetic and caring. Over dinner she never hogged the conversation but neither did she expect to be entertained. Good talkers, she knew, did not necessarily make good writers; in some cases it signalled the opposite. In Soho pubs in the 1950s and 1960s she had encountered countless self-styled poets and novelists who when drunk would talk as if they were on the cusp of writing a great book but who, more often than not, never got round to producing one.

In Tuscany, Muriel's circle was wide and varied and included expatriates from around the globe as well as many native Italians. Often, to coincide with my arrival, she would arrange a gathering of friends at San Giovanni or in a restaurant or at friends' houses. Everyone was happy to travel a couple of hours on such occasions, from Cortona or Lucca or Florence, eighty kilometres away on the frantic autostrada. In those days no one was inhibited by the consequences of drinking and driving. Mostly, the assembled company was of Muriel's vintage, drawn to Italy in the aftermath of the Second World War for the lifestyle, climate and culture, and the comparative cheapness of living.

Lunch, usually at a restaurant, was the focal point of the day. It was, as I discovered, a daunting proposition. It comprised five courses, starting with *antipasto* and followed by the *primo* (soup or pasta), the *secondo* (chicken, meat or fish), the *contorno* (vegetables), the *dolce* (dessert) or *formaggio* (cheese), and *caffè*. Wine was served routinely, and grappa or limoncello were offered as digestifs. To attempt to avoid one or more courses was not acceptable and invited the opprobrium of restaurateurs who gave the impression that to do so was somehow a mark of disrespect. Since shops and other businesses closed at one o'clock and did not open again until four, there was no need to rush. The fast food revolution had yet to reach Tuscany. Once, in Florence, as I made my way through the courses, I ordered *ribollita*, a potage of leftover vegetables – cabbage being a mainstay – and day-old bread. It literally means re-boiled, which may not sound all that appetising but when well made it is utterly delicious. I knew that it was unwise to keep on eating it – for there was chicken cacciatore and *patate arroste* still to come, not to mention *tiramisu* – but it was so moreish that I couldn't help myself. On and on I ploughed until I felt that if I was pricked with a pin I would explode. Of the dishes that came in its wake I have no recollection. I do remember, though, that when I got back to my hotel I went immediately to bed and did not wake up until the next morning.

Italy was a place where art was part of daily routine. It was in the fabric and facades of the buildings and in the way towns and villages seemed naturally to blend with their surroundings. Aestheticism was instinctive, a common trait, as if it were one of the senses. Artfulness was ubiquitous, from the wrapping of one's purchases in a shop to the arrangement of food on a plate. The most common word in the language appeared to be *bella*, which prefixed everything from the morning espresso to the design of a dress. Great effort – and great importance – was placed on how things looked. Tuscany's landscape was the ultimate expression of this. It was the view that travellers dreamt of, composed who knew how by diverse hands over centuries. It even smelled wonderful, of clean air and woodsmoke, of rosemary and new leather, of frying garlic and pungent *parmigiano*.

The majority of Muriel's friends – *stranieri* as the natives called them – were in permanent residence but a few were peripatetic, coming and going as commitments permitted. Long gone, however, and much mourned, were Italophiles of a previous generation, such as the aesthetes Harold Acton and John Pope-Hennessy, the writer Joan Haslip, William 'Bill' Weaver – translator of *The Name of the Rose* among many other books – and Alan Pryce-Jones, erstwhile editor of the *Times Literary Supplement*. It was hard not to sense the ending of an era. In their stead Muriel and Penny had accumulated a number of new and exotic friends whom they saw with familial regularity. One was Thekla Clark. Originally from Oklahoma, she personified the pioneering spirit with what she described as her 'New World exuberance and vulgarity'. Nothing and no one appeared to faze her. When Thekla was around there were no uncomfortable silences, no conversational lacunae. She was in awe of Muriel, to whom she happily deferred. When I first met her she lived in a tower at Bagno a Ripoli that was once part of the defences of Florence, with her husband John, co-creator of Società Scala, the first photographic colour archive of works of art. Over lunch one day John told me that he arrived in Florence in 1949 to study Renaissance philosophy and art history. Prior to that he had attended an American college to do a course in 'The Hundred Great Books', an idea I thought well worth resuscitating.

Within a few minutes of meeting Thekla she told me that she had been a friend of W. H. Auden whom she had met in the 1950s in Ischia. Rumours that she had slept with him, she said, were, like reports of Mark Twain's death, greatly exaggerated. Auden, however, had been sufficiently attached to her to propose marriage, which Thekla – described by one of the poet's biographers as 'an elegant and generous young American woman' – had respectfully declined. No damage was done to their friendship, about which she wrote in a fond memoir. Thekla's Florentine first husband, her 'noble Italian lover', had died young. She then had a daughter, Lisa, whose father was killed by a hit-and-run driver in Los Angeles before she could get to know him.

In 1961, Thekla and John were married and had a son, Simon. Throughout the 1960s the couple were increasingly concerned over American involvement in south-east Asia. However, rather than merely voice protest, they wanted to do something tangible. When in 1975 Saigon fell and they saw photographs of Vietnamese clinging to helicopters taking Americans to safety they could wait no longer. After several frustrating years, they finally managed to 'adopt' an ethnically Chinese refugee family from Vietnam. Less than a year later, the Clarks added four members of a Cambodian family to their household. They arrived with everything they owned: a few clothes, a wooden mortar and pestle, and a Bible. Thekla, an instinctive bohemian, welcomed these 'boat people' like the open-hearted landlady of a gratis B&B. She and John were pragmatic idealists.

Near Montevarchi, in the commune of Arezzo, lived the Australian painter Jeffrey Smart and his partner Ermes De Zan. On my arrival at San Giovanni late one freezing February Muriel said that Jeffrey had invited us all to supper at La Posticcia Nuova, the expansive farmhouse that he had acquired in a dilapidated state in the 1970s since when it had been sensitively restored. We reached it in inky darkness,

Muriel, a 'constitutional exile', in Arezzo in 1986

the night sky sparkling with stars like a jeweller's window. Fat logs spat and crackled in the blackened fireplace, on both sides of which were packed bookcases. Jeffrey's paintings, into which he sometimes inserted himself Hitchcock-like, were of underground car parks, container terminals, storage units and truckers' stops, situations as alien to Tuscany as the moon. While Ermes offered hors d'oeuvres, Jeffrey talked about T. S. Eliot, many of whose poems he had learned off by heart. He was an omnivorous reader and numbered among his friends Germaine Greer and Clive James, both of whom he had painted portraits of. He said that, of late, he had been reading Aldous Huxley. 'I believe he was an admirer of yours, Muriel, wasn't he?' he said. Muriel did not immediately respond. Then, just when it seemed she was not going to comment, she said: 'Why wouldn't he be?' It was said without a hint of arrogance but it did take Jeffrey aback. On such occasions Ermes would top up glasses and change the topic of conversation to his own immediate concerns. Although he had studied art, he had opted not to pursue painting as a career; two powerful egos under the same roof was one too many. Instead he ran the house and tended the land attached to La Posticcia Nuova. He had a flock of sheep, Suffolks, which kept the grass from growing out of control and he had planted groves of olives whose oil he sold. Even so Jeffrey and he managed to travel and every summer they went to Bayreuth for Wagner's *Ring Cycle*.

Among Muriel's other friends was Alain Vidal Naquet. Born in Paris, Alain was a delightful, gentle man, a diplomat, who had retired to Cortona after working for the World Food Council at the United Nations. He was a writer manqué and asked for advice which I was ill-equipped to give. I said that he could do a lot worse than follow the prescription Mrs Hawkins gives to authors in *A Far Cry from Kensington*, which is to write as if you're sending a letter to a dear and close friend: 'Write privately, not publicly; without fear or timidity, right to the end of the letter, as if it was never going to be published, so that your true friend will read it over and over, and then want more enchanting letters from you.' Once, at supper I was introduced to Benedetta Origo. She was the elder daughter of Iris Origo, whose wonderful book, *War in Val D'Orcia*, records how she and her husband, Antonio, revived the fortunes of their Tuscan estate, La Foce, with its more than fifty farms and 7,000 acres. The war had split Italy, pitting fathers against sons, brothers against brothers. It was a civil war within a global one. Bravely, the Origos offered sanctuary to partisans and fugitive Allied prisoners-of-war. Benedetta was a toddler when, in the midst of shells falling and the sound of gunfire, the family had to leave their home and belongings and seek refuge in nearby Montepulciano. After Iris died in 1988, aged eighty-six, Benedetta and her sister Donata took over the running of La Foce. How much of Tuscany does Benedetta own? I asked Muriel. 'How far can the eye see?' she replied.

There were, of course, a number of English expatriates living in what became known in the 1980s as Chiantishire. Notable among them was John Mortimer, former barrister and creator of Rumpole of the Bailey. Most summers he and his wife would rent a house in the area and visit Muriel and Penny at San Giovanni, bringing with them whoever happened to be their guests. One year Neil and Glenda Kinnock tagged along. Penny recalled how, in order to deposit John, who was having trouble walking, as near as possible to the alfresco dining area, Neil insisted on driving their hired car through a narrow side gate which even she – who could park a tank in a space reserved for a Vespa – would have hesitated to attempt. To the suggestion that this might be unwise, the erstwhile leader of the Labour Party replied that he had better get through it or he was not the European Commissioner for Transport. In John's opinion Muriel was 'our best novelist' bar none. Visiting in the blistering heat of August 1997, he found her recovering from a hip operation that had not gone to plan. If she was in pain, which she surely was, she did not allow it to spoil the fun. She and Penny had recently been to church, they told him, where the priest, apparently oblivious to the reproductive capabilities of his ageing parishioners, had railed against the use of contraception.

John's popular comic novel *Summer's Lease*, published in 1988, encouraged yet more visitors to Tuscany. At its core is the so-called Piero della Francesca Trail, which can be completed in one hectic day. After an early breakfast, the first stop is Arezzo and the fresco cycle *Legend of the True Cross* in the chancel of the Basilica of San Francesca. It may be one of the great Renaissance masterpieces but it does not detain the fictional tourists for long. 'Not ten o'clock yet', remarks one, 'and we've done Arezzo. It won't take us long to knock off the pregnant Madonna.' Much restored, she – 'so far gone in pregnancy that her dress . . . will not fasten' – is to be found at Monterchi, which lies twenty kilometres away. All that's required to appreciate this gem is a few minutes, then off the tourists trot to Sansepolcro, Piero's birthplace, where the main attraction is *The Resurrection*, which they intend to 'do' before lunch, notwithstanding Aldous Huxley's claim that it is 'the greatest picture in the world'. The final stop on the itinerary is Urbino. The road from Tuscany into Umbria climbs steeply and twists round hairpin bends over the 'Alpe Della Luna – the Mountains of the Moon' – towards the sea and Piero's *Dream of St Jerome*, which is known more

Piero della Francesca's *Madonna del Parto* – the pregnant Madonna – in Monterchi. Muriel liked it because it was 'peasant-like and noble'

popularly as *The Flagellation*. Here, as John Pope-Hennessy pointed out, John Mortimer's interpretation of the painting, which he believed to depict the flagellation of Christ overseen by Pontius Pilate, goes comically awry. As Pope-Hennessy observed: 'there is no Christ, no Pontius Pilate, indeed no real flagellation'. What it does depict is the dream St Jerome had as a young man in which he was flayed for reading pagan texts.

Muriel's favourite of these paintings was the pregnant Madonna – *Madonna del Parto* – which, when she first took me to see it, was the sole work in a tiny cemetery chapel in Monterchi. She liked it, she said, because it was 'peasant-like and noble'. To Muriel the Virgin was both the protagonist of a play and its setting, 'as she opens her dress to prepare for the historic curtain-rise of the Incarnation'. I have lost count of the number of times she and Penny and I journeyed to Monterchi, either from Sansepolcro or on the way there. It was easy to imagine that you were in a countryside unchanged since Piero's day, the roads lined with chestnut and cypress trees. The longevity of cypresses is legendary. Some of them, it's been estimated, may be as old as 2,000 years. Noah's Ark was made from cypress wood, or so the Bible says.

Muriel and Penny were full of such facts and stories. As we bowled along they would relate tales from local newspapers, the gorier the better: suspicious deaths, unsolved murders and crimes of passion. Near San Giovanni is the 'castle-hamlet' – as Muriel described it – of Gargonza, with a spectacular view of the Val di Chiana. It is surrounded by dense woods in which roam herds of wild boar, the prey of hunters, garbed like commandos, who pursue them with dogs and rifles. The hunting season begins officially on the first Sunday in September and ends on the last day of February. Throughout this period the sound of gunfire can often be heard puncturing the countryside's quiet. The hunters protect their 'rights' assiduously and, often, nefariously and illegally. In Tuscany alone there are estimated to be around 130,000 hunters, virtually all of whom are male. While it may be legitimate to keep in check the number of wild boar in order to stop them destroying crops it is less easy to defend the slaughter of birds, many species of which until recently were hunted almost to extinction. Hunters go to extraordinary lengths to kill these harmless creatures. Some build blinds – trenches at ground level that enable them to remain hidden – or hide in woodlands. Others use caged singing birds to attract the wild birds within shot. They also lay traps and put down poison in order to kill cats and dogs which, they insist, interfere with the repopulation of wildlife after the hunting season closes. But, as Muriel said: 'This is a lot of rot. There is no game left to repopulate.'

Over the years she and Penny lost numerous cats and dogs to poison. First to succumb was Pavoncino, a part-Dalmatian mongrel. One morning, Muriel recalled, she was sitting for a portrait in the deconsecrated church which Penny used as a studio. Pavoncino bounded in to see them before taking off on his daily romp. He was never seen again. Raoul, another mongrel, rescued from a rubbish dump, ate poisoned bait – meat stuffed with strychnine – and expired in the garden. Similar fates befell Algy and Mungo, the two hunting hounds which Muriel and Penny had when I first knew them. Then, against their better instincts, they adopted Shadow, who turned up at the door one day starving and in need of veterinary attention. He, too, was found in the undergrowth, poisoned, after he escaped from his run. Somehow, he survived. Muriel was determined to highlight the ugly reality of the Tuscan idyll and, when two dogs owned by her friend, the journalist Alexander Chancellor, were poisoned, she wrote an uncompromising article for an Italian newspaper. As a consequence, as Penny told me: 'They all hate her, it's been marvellous.' In one article, Muriel wrote: 'People ask me why I stay in Italy in these circumstances, why don't I move somewhere more kindly disposed towards the animals I love to be with? I can only say that Italy is Europe. I am altogether a European. The slaughter of animals and extinction of birds is a European problem. Besides, although I am 81, I am very tough; I am not a quitter.'

The Piazza Navona, Rome. Muriel had an apartment in a palazzo which had once housed the library of Cardinal Orsini

4

SEEKING WITH NEW EYES

A scenario is a garble. A bad one is a bungle. They need not be
plausible, only hypnotic, like all good art.

THE ABBESS OF CREWE

Muriel first met Penny in Rome in the spring of 1968.
The venue was a hairdressing salon in Via Santa Maria
dell'Anima. Penny was at art school and on the lookout for
a secretarial job to tide her over. For her part Muriel, having
escaped New York with its caterwauling and claustrophobia,
was in need of an assistant, someone who could look after her
correspondence and keep her papers in order. She was content to
be in Rome, at least in the beginning. An unknown place always
held the possibility for her of reinvention and renewal, even of
metamorphosis. Moreover, Rome felt like home, spiritually,
culturally and temperamentally. It was the city of her faith,
where that ardent Italophile Miss Brodie was wont to spend her
summer holidays and where she claimed – ever the spinner of
truth-testing tales – to have had an audience with the Pope. There
was an embarrassment of shops, galleries, churches, restaurants.
And there was always something to do and interesting people –
Gore Vidal, Anthony Burgess, countless counts and contessas,
a plethora of princes and princesses. It could sometimes seem
that there were few Italians who did not have a title, which both
amused and bemused Muriel; in Scotland you could go a lifetime
without encountering a Lord or a laird. She loved dressing up
and eating out. She was a dedicated follower of haute couture, a

religious reader of *Vogue*, and a keen appraiser of *la bella figura*. But if that suggests she was resting on her laurels and taking a break it would be misleading. Writing was what spurred her on. 'That's all I ever really wanted to do, write stories and novels,' she told one interviewer, recalling her time in the Eternal City. 'That's when I'm at my happiest.'

Whenever she was close to finishing a book she would have herself admitted to the Salvator Mundi hospital, which she came to regard as a sort of writing retreat. Surrounded by greenery and located at the top of the Gianicolo Hill, it was off the beaten track, sepulchrally quiet with panoramic views of Rome and nearby villages. A doctor friend signed her in, though more often than not there was nothing medically wrong with her. The nuns who ran the hospital much preferred their patients to be free of ailments; they couldn't be bothered with anyone who was actually unwell. Or such was Muriel's impression. Among her fellow patients were self-obsessed celebrities seeking a cosmetic solution to their perceived imperfections or a cure for their addictions. The Pope was believed to use the hospital though Muriel never bumped into him in the public areas unless, she speculated, he was in disguise. 'I would take a private room,' she once told me, pooh-poohing the notion that it was an odd thing to do. 'It was quite cheap, and I could disappear from sight where no one could get at me.'

Muriel suggested this was advice that I – or anyone else for that matter – might follow. Another of her recommendations was that if you want to lose weight it might not be a bad idea to eat less, with which most dietitians would concur. Yet another wise saw was that when you find yourself in trouble you should go immediately to Paris, where an infusion of *joie de vivre* will do you the world of good. One of my favourites was: 'Never

pour with your left hand, that was the one the Borgias used.'
She was always eager to pass on such pearls of wisdom, a trait
which I suspected she inherited from her mother. It was Cissy
Camberg, for example, who said that if you didn't learn how
to do housework you would never be called upon to do any.
No one accepted this fiat as enthusiastically as Muriel. Once,
as Penny related, she did attempt to make a bed, which led to
cracked ribs. Quite how this happened was never explained. On
another occasion when Muriel was in hospital for an operation
she came round from the anaesthetic to find her young
Calabrian maid sitting on the floor eating a bun. How typical
of Italy, she said, where 'all your family and friends come into
hospital to chase away the bugs and find out what they're doing
to you'. I've often thought she would have made a wonderful, if
somewhat unconventional, agony aunt.

Her stay in Rome was creatively fecund. There, she wrote
The Public Image and much of *The Takeover*. Among her several
residences was an apartment in a palazzo which had once housed
the library of Cardinal Orsini, who in the fifteenth century
may have been poisoned by Cesare Borgia, a grisly detail that
undoubtedly added to its appeal. The apartment was tastefully if
sparsely furnished with Persian carpets, a cavernous fireplace and
what seemed to be an empty acre of polished floor. If she wanted
to take some exercise, she said, she had no need to go outside for
a stroll; all she need do was walk from one end of the room to
the other. It was a perfect space for a party and Muriel threw a
lot of them; in more senses than one she was a born entertainer.

Penny was in some respects Muriel's opposite. Her family
was well-connected. Jessie, her mother, was a Macpherson,
from Glen Urquhart in Inverness- shire. She was known, Penny
recalled, as 'an heiress' though the basis for this was unclear. Her

Muriel in Rome in 1969. Unlike Miss Jean Brodie she never had an audience with the Pope

father, Sir Douglas Jardine, came from a long line of doctors. He was also a Scot, albeit one born in London, and was educated at Westminster School and Trinity College, Cambridge. On his death in December 1946, *The Times* described him as 'A Notable Colonial Administrator'. He was the author of a much-praised book called *The Mad Mullah of Somaliland* – the sobriquet of Mohammed Abdullah Hassan, leader of the Dervish – who it was said royally entertained 'infidels' before roasting them like hogs over a slow fire. It was to Sir Douglas's relief that he had never been the guest of 'His Madness'. Muriel, unlike Penny, read his book and enjoyed it, especially the observation that 'camel's milk was not half bad laced with rum'.

While her father flitted around far-flung parts of a contracting Empire – Cyprus, Somaliland, Abyssinia, Nigeria, Tanganyika, Sierra Leone and the Leeward Islands featured among his postings – Penny attended boarding school in England and finishing school in Switzerland. Following the sudden deaths of her mother in 1943, and her father three years later at the age of fifty-eight, she was brought up by guardians. In the midst of the Second World War, she and her sister, with her mother and father, had to make a perilous crossing of the Atlantic. Their vessel was part of a convoy which was attacked simultaneously by German planes and U-boats. Penny never forgot standing on the middle deck of the besieged boat, holding hands with her terrified mother whose face, she said, was the pallor of pure fear.

Earlier in the war, when her father, as Governor of Sierra Leone, received a message from the enemy side, suggesting that if he wanted to save his life he should follow their instructions and put the forces at his command where they told him to. The Germans were then in North Africa and eager to advance south and expand their reach, hoping to link the conquered territory to colonies which had been lost at the end of the First World War. It was an offer Sir Douglas was never likely to accept but he recognised that it presented an opportunity too good to pass up. He contacted the Foreign Office, insisting he had a plan for bringing the war to a swift conclusion. He would express interest in what had been outlined but would ask to discuss the deal personally with Hitler. Certain that the Führer had not had yellow fever, from which Sir Douglas himself had recovered, he suggested that he attend the meeting with a box of Swan Vesta matches packed with yellow fever germs. As he and Hitler talked, he would fill up his pipe, produce the matchbox and release the lethal germs. Hitler would catch yellow fever and die faster than you could say 'Sieg Heil!'. The Foreign Office replied with an unequivocal 'No'. They had never heard of a more stupid idea. Furthermore, it 'wouldn't be cricket' to dispatch the genocidal dictator in such an unsporting manner.

Penny was an accomplished painter and sculptor, though you would never have known it from talking to her for she was the definition of modest. Sculpture appealed to her, she said, because there were better models at the Florentine Accademia and she chose to go there. She and Muriel were simpatico and complemented each other. They were comfortable in their own company and travelled long distances. All of Europe was theirs to explore. They would travel hundreds of miles to visit a museum or gallery or hear a piece of music. Once, on the way to England, they got as far as Boulogne before changing their minds and returning to Tuscany. For Muriel, travelling was how she replenished her store of experience. 'Nothing', she once said, 'can be done without it.' One of her favourite quotes was from Proust: 'the real voyage of discovery consists not in seeking new lands, but in seeking with new eyes'. Muriel took this as her credo. It was, she said on receiving the David Cohen Prize in 1997, the 'ultimate truth, never to be overlooked. But it has surely to be qualified by the likelihood that "new eyes" are very greatly stimulated by new faces, new sights and sounds.' To her, travel was literature's lifeblood: 'We have to find at first hand how other people live and die, what they smell, how they are made. I recommend travel to young authors. And also to authors not so young.'

Journalists who interviewed Muriel would find Penny at her side, which a few resented. There was the assumption by some that they were lesbians rather than simply companions. One, ludicrously, described Penny as Muriel's 'Dragon' whose role it was to protect her from unwelcome intrusions. It was the kind of observation that could only have been made by someone who did not know them. Muriel was eminently capable of repelling anyone she did not want to see or associate with. The plain fact was that the arrangement was mutually beneficial. Muriel had at least five rooms at San Giovanni that she could call her own. But she had no desire to live alone. From her experience as a writer, she said, she had to spend long hours every day in silence if not in solitude. She appreciated that not everyone could cope with this: 'but I have always sought the company of those who understand my need'. No one was more understanding or sympathetic than Penny. San Giovanni's isolation helped create the impression that she and Muriel were reclusive. With its shutters closed, stout door firmly locked and large dogs barking frenziedly, it was as forbidding as a Border keep. Unheralded visitors would be greeted by Penny crying – humorously – 'Friend or foe?' from the kitchen window on the first floor. As I approached the house, in the midst of winter, say, or with a lightning storm forking in a pewter-coloured sky, I was reminded of the bleak and ruinous House of Shaws in Robert Louis Stevenson's *Kidnapped*, which was required reading in Muriel's childhood: 'Blood built it; blood stopped the building of it; blood shall bring it down.'

It was in the summer of 1975 that Muriel finally decided to forsake Rome for Oliveto. At the time she was writing *The Takeover*, which was causing her more bother than she was used to having with a novel. When the book was finished she and Penny took it to Arezzo to have it photocopied. It was late and the shop was about to close but the young man in charge agreed to work overtime to complete the job. 'We were staying at the Hotel Continentale,' remembered Penny, 'and Muriel woke at 5 a.m. and said, "I must go over the road and see how my book is doing." We got there just in time; the manuscript had caught fire! Somewhere I should have one of the scorched pages, which I kept as a souvenir. The poor boy was almost fired for wrecking the machine.'

Muriel's writing routine was as ritualised as Catholicism's daily observances. She was not an early riser, seldom reaching her desk before eleven o'clock. She did not write more than one draft, nor was there much in the way of editing or correcting. Clarity of thought and expression was her aim. Before starting to write she would research her subject or theme deeply and discursively, requesting help as and when necessary. 'I take a lot of time before I strike,' she said. Having been a reference librarian in a previous existence I was always happy to offer my services as a researcher.

For *Aiding and Abetting*, which has as its backdrop the case of Lord Lucan, who disappeared without trace after murdering his children's nanny whom he mistook for his wife, I sent newspaper cuttings detailing how his son was trying to have his father declared dead. 'Please send all the up-to-date info you have,' Muriel requested. While working on *Reality and Dreams*, she asked for whatever I was able to find on the subject of redundancy, especially as it affected the lives of individuals. For *The Finishing School* she wanted everything I could lay my hands on about Mary, Queen of Scots, including copies of the controversial Casket Letters, which it is said were written by the tragic monarch and which were used against her by the traitorous Scots lords. Among my books I found an eye-witness account of Mary's execution, which I offered to Muriel. 'I hate to deprive you of it,' she replied immediately. 'Is it short enough to photocopy?'

How what I sent influenced her novels was not immediately apparent to me on reading the finished product, but she was always effusive in her gratitude. She wrote by hand using a fountain pen. Like many writers, she fetishised the implements of her trade. Her notebooks – 'The Bothwell Spiral' – in which she wrote her novels, came from the Edinburgh bookseller and stationer James Thin. One notebook contained around 10,000 words. Thus she could tell how many were required to make a book. The manuscript of *The Prime of Miss Jean Brodie*, which is lodged in the University of Tulsa, runs to just four notebooks. As soon as the manuscript was ready it was turned over to Penny for typing. When on song, when it flowed, Muriel could write a novel in a matter of weeks, sometimes writing throughout the night. *The Prime of Miss Jean Brodie*, for example, took her a month and a half. The way she described the process made it seem no more troublesome than taking down dictation; she knew what she wanted to say and how she wanted to say it. She was in control of the tap and all she need do was turn it on. Not, of course, that she was immune to what Penny described – vis-à-vis *The Finishing School* – as every artist's self-doubt: 'Will it still be O.K. at the next reading? Will some part of the plot stick

Chapter One

The boys, as they talked to the girls from ~~Haven~~ Maurice Blaine school, stood on the far side of their bicycles, holding the handlebars, ~~so that there~~ which established was a protective fence of bicycle between the sexes, and ~~at the same time a sense of an~~ ~~saw~~ the impression that at any moment they ~~the boys~~ were ~~likely~~ to ~~mount their bicycles and~~ be off. away.

The girls could not take off their panama hats because this was not far from the school gates and hatlessness was an offence. But certain departures from the proper set of the ~~hat in their~~ hat on the head were overlooked in the case of fourth-form girls and upward, ~~although whilst as~~ so long as nobody ~~were set~~ ~~the proper arrangement of the brim was up at the back and their hat at an angle. the p But there~~ ~~down at the front~~ were other subtle variants from the ordinary rule of ~~brim up wearing~~ the brim turned up at the back and down at the front. The five

A James Thin notebook manuscript page from *The Prime of Miss Jean Brodie* out from another bit? Has that character changed their name on page 49? Will the publisher like it? Will the reviewers trash it? Will any readers ever buy it? And so on . . .'

'I'd like to make a classic. Why not?' This was Muriel's response to the plan hatched by BBC Scotland in 1995 to make a documentary about her. It was a tricky negotiation, with me playing the part of go-between. At first Muriel seemed eager then she was less so. Her health was not good; faxes would arrive from a medical centre in Essex detailing her many illnesses. When not seeing a physiotherapist she was having X-rays. On top of which she was popping antibiotics as if they were Polo mints: 'I have to swallow over 20 antibiotics a day to combat the massive infection I harbour in my hip.' As ever, her latest novel, which at the time was *Reality and Dreams*, was her priority. Just when it seemed that filming would proceed as scheduled, Muriel decided she must devote all her energy to completing the book. It was with 'a heavy heart' she wrote that she must postpone the proposed programme, adding: 'I can only offer to get in touch the moment I am fairly clear of my novel . . .'

A few days later, however, following a plea from the director, Eleanor Yule, Muriel changed her mind and agreed to allow filming to go ahead, which it did at San Giovanni in September of that year. The weather was lovely: not too hot with a soothing breeze. Muriel and Penny were welcoming hosts, and their maid, Patrizia, made lasagne for lunch. My interview with Muriel, which formed the spine of the programme, took place in her part of the house, her back to an open window from which the whole of the Val di Chiana spread out like a verdant counterpane. She had a summer cold, and her eyes were rheumy, but still she sparkled like a diamond in a tiara. She may have had the body of a sedentary septuagenarian but her mind was alert.

In preparation for the film she requested that I give her some idea of the questions I might ask. She didn't want to spoil the spontaneity of the interview, she said, 'but perhaps a preliminary dialogue will not go amiss'. I asked first about the subject of death which I suggested was pervasive throughout her work. It was, she responded, 'every novelist's subject'. *Memento Mori* was her specific book on the subject. 'But this and other novels are different interpretatively from most other novels.' Her career as a novelist, she added, had coincided with her conversion to Catholicism. She had studied St Thomas Aquinas and his methods of interpretation – 'historical (or literal), allegorical, anagogical (or spiritual), symbolical and mystical'. She had written books on all five levels. She also read the English mystics and Cardinal Newman, whose prose she thought 'superb'. Another influence was the French novelist André Gide, especially his novel *Les Faux Monnayeurs*, which was translated into English as *The Counterfeiters*. 'I could see how the type you call "blackmailers, thieves, two-faced schemers" could be liberated in literature from their prototypian villainous parts without ceasing to be villains.'

Another question concerned ghosts. Did she believe in them? She did, she said, 'in the sense of atmosphere'. She had had no psychic experience herself and certainly did not subscribe to the idea of ghosts 'clanking about old houses'. What interested her was the 'unexplained'. As for form, it afforded her the opportunity to experiment. But she did not experiment for the sake of it; it was with 'the precise intention' of making a point.

'I have for instance flash-forwards as well as flash-backs. This actually intensifies suspense in a paradoxical way. Readers want to know how such and such a thing happened and the stated fact that it happened serves to whet curiosity. I am constantly aware of the reader while I am writing. I am concerned with what the effect I am writing will be on the reader. The "reader" is a person in a chair with a book.' She had no idea when writing a book how it might turn out. Its theme built of itself and if did not develop, it ramified. I wanted to know what she saw as her achievement, her legacy. 'I have realised myself,' she replied, 'I have expressed something I brought into the world with me. I have liberated the novel in many ways, shown how anything whatever can be narrated, any experience set down, including sheer damn cheek. I think I have opened doors and windows in the mind, and challenged fears – especially the most inhibiting fears about what a novel should be.'

I asked about her mother and what influence she might have had on her. Very little, she said, though she remembered her as 'very positive' and that she welcomed all of Muriel's friends. She liked to sing the popular songs of the day and recited nursery rhymes and told fairy stories. She was always on the go and never silent. Thinking of her childhood, Muriel had come to appreciate that she knew at the time she was 'living through material for later nostalgia. I would look at sunlight on a wall for a long time, consciously storing it up.' Her school days were engrained in her memory. James Gillespie's, she now saw, was a far more progressive school than she had been aware of when she was a pupil. 'So it seems to me when I compare my school experience with other people of my age – people who went to good English schools for instance. It was always said that Scottish education was the best in the world. Whether that was true or not we had a sense of educational privilege.' It always irritated her when people said she was English, and she would always correct them: 'No, Scottish.' But she felt blessed that her first language was English which, she felt, was unrivalled in its expressiveness. It was to a writer what Carrara marble is to a sculptor. Having said that, she could find nothing in English literature to exceed the Scottish border ballads.

On return from Tuscany, editing of the film began. Contrary to Muriel's wishes an interview had taken place with Eugene Walter, an American whom she had known when she first moved to Rome. A flamboyantly gay gadfly, Walter, whose nickname was 'Tum-te-tum', a catchphrase he claimed as his own, hailed from Mobile, Alabama. An assiduous networker, he seemed to know and cultivate everyone from Judy Garland and Anaïs Nin to Gore Vidal and William Faulkner. In his childhood, he had been friends with Truman Capote. A jack-of-all-trades, he had contributed to the *Paris Review* in its infancy and translated scripts for Federico Fellini, in several of whose movies he appeared, notably 8½, in which he played the American journalist. Initially, he had been helpful to Muriel but latterly there had been a falling out and all contact had ended. Whatever had occasioned the fracture it must have been serious for, subsequently – as Martin Stannard, Muriel's official biographer, noted – Walter was 'verbally electrocuted' by her.

When she learned that the BBC had spoken to him and intended to feature him in the film, she was livid. As Eleanor Yule acknowledged, 'The shit has hit the fan . . .' In a letter to her, Muriel let rip. Walter, she said, 'held the nearest thing to a salon'. He was the 'unofficial reception committee and all roads led to him'. He had been of some service to her – on the subject of cats, upholstery and such-like – but little more. 'He got paid for it,' Muriel added. 'Paid too well.' When she went into hospital for a serious operation – a hysterectomy – he did not visit her and she did not hear from him for over ten years. 'It seems to me,' she concluded, 'you have got hold of the wrong person. I have been troubled throughout my life by one mythomaniac [Derek Stanford] and do not propose my biography to be distorted by another of those.' After the appropriate apologies, Walter's contribution to the film was shelved.

The Elusive Spark was broadcast in the spring of 1996 and was generally well received. When I asked Muriel what she thought of it she said she liked everything about it 'except myself'. In his diary, the actor Alec Guinness gave his impression of it, and of its subject:

> In the evening we watched an excellent TV interview with Dame Muriel Spark. She came over as wonderfully direct, honest, witty and charming. When she lived in Rome some years ago she invited us to drinks in her splendid apartment. At that time she wore her hair piled high; there were flashing jewels and chic clothes, and she was most affable. The last time I saw her was in June 1991, at the memorial service for Graham Greene. We sat next to each other; we were both required to get up and speak. She wore no make-up and was almost casually dressed. In her tribute to Graham she spoke of the financial help he gave her when she was a struggling writer. She said, 'It was typical of Graham that with the monthly cheques he would often send a few bottles of wine to "take the edge off cold charity".' It says something very pleasing about both of them.

As her eightieth birthday approached, Muriel's body was like that of an old banger which can no longer get up steep hills or overtake pedestrians and which invariably fails its annual MOT. Parts constantly needed to be replaced or repaired. Her letters made light of her manifold woes. Her main concern was that every time something went awry it impeded her ability to work and swallowed precious hours. A nurse called twice daily at San Giovanni to administer injections which alleviated the pain and allowed Muriel to return to her desk. I was often reminded of *Memento Mori*, her sublime comedy about ageing, written when she was forty. 'Being over seventy is like being engaged in a war,' remarks one character. 'All our friends are going or gone and we survive among the dead and the dying as on a battlefield.' Another character says that if he were to go to Heaven and find Dylan Thomas there, he'd prefer to go to Hell.

Muriel's response to her catalogue of ailments was to carry on regardless as far as possible. If she needed patching up, so be it. But she was damned if it was going to floor her. The celebrations for her significant anniversary proceeded apace. Not without justification Penny called it Babette's Feast, after the movie of the same name in which a former chef living as a humble servant wins the lottery and spends it all on a sumptuous meal for her employers. Babette's generosity, like Muriel's, is boundless and uncontrolled. Ultimately, however, it proves efficacious: friendships are renewed, old sores healed and a once joyless community now brims with joy. 'We already have a store of champagne,' Penny wrote to me, 'and the house is already upside-down, which Muriel is taking very well considering she can no longer get to her study and when she does it is a sea of armchairs, carpets rolled up and nuts and bolts.' In response to my offer to be of help, Penny replied: 'perhaps you can, pouring libations'.

In the event, no help was needed. I arrived on the appointed day, 1 February, at noon to find numerous waiters shuffling around purposefully like penguins on parade: arranging tables, setting places, polishing glasses. Muriel, in her outsized owlish, designer-label spectacles, surveyed the scene with a look of astonishment. She had accepted the offer of an Italian friend to organise the whole event, she said, and 'It's all got a bit out of control.' There were twenty or so guests for a lunch that lasted through the afternoon and into the evening. Her American publisher, Barbara Epler, came from New York, as did the literary agent Robin Straus with her husband, the novelist Joseph Kanon. The hot topic of conversation was Bill Clinton's fling with Monica Lewinsky and his weasel-worded excuse: 'I did not have sexual relations with that woman.' It took Muriel back to the era of Watergate and Deep Throat, and *The Abbess of Crewe*, her inspired take on that unholy scandal. Later those of us who were staying at San Giovanni watched on Muriel's enormous television CNN's coverage of the latest twist in the Clinton debâcle. Would the Senate dare to impeach him? As we grazed on leftovers and sipped nightcaps – who would have thought that Brussels sprouts and brandy would go well together? – Muriel argued that the embattled president could not be guilty of adultery *and* lying because lying is part of adultery. The two were umbilically attached and could not be disassociated. Thus, I could not help but think, was the seed of fiction planted.

Downtown Manhattan, near the headquarters of the *New Yorker*, in whose pages
The Prime of Miss Jean Brodie first appeared

5
MANHATTAN REVISITED

*New York, home of the vivisectors of the mind, and of the mentally
vivisected still to be reassembled, of those who live intact, habitually
wondering about their states of sanity, . . .*

THE HOTHOUSE BY THE EAST RIVER

It is sometimes assumed that Muriel's association with the
New Yorker began in 1961 with *The Prime of Miss Jean Brodie*.
In fact, it can be traced to a couple of years before then. She had
been on the magazine's radar for some time and had been asked
to submit stories for consideration which, though always read
with interest and appreciation, invariably met with regretful
rejection. The breakthrough came in 1960 when the magazine
accepted 'The Ormolu Clock'. Not long afterwards she agreed
to let it have initial sight of everything she wrote. In *New Yorker*-
speak this was called a 'first reading' agreement, which Muriel
later dubbed a 'cross-breeding' agreement. Under these terms,
a select group of writers gave the *New Yorker* first refusal of
all their work for which they would be given a twenty-five per
cent bonus on top of the usual fee for anything it did decide to
publish. It was an arrangement that continued to the mutual
benefit of both parties until Muriel's death, forty-seven years
later.

When Muriel began writing for it, the *New Yorker* was
widely regarded as one of the best magazines in the world.
Founded in 1925, it had a reputation for fine writing, urbane
commentary, accurate reporting – its fact-checkers had a

formidable, Torquemada-like reputation – and inspired cartoons. Its tone was set by the original editor, Harold Ross, who nurtured a stable of thoroughbred wits in the manner of a trainer who is never happy even when leading one of his steeds into the winner's enclosure. As one rueful writer recalled, 'Only perfection was good enough for him, and on the rare occasions he encountered it, he viewed it with astonished suspicion.'

Among Ross's earliest contributors were James Thurber, Dorothy Parker, Robert Benchley and E. B. White. It fell to Thurber to be his first memorialiser and mythologiser. In *The Years With Ross*, published in 1957, he portrayed the irascible and unpredictable editor as an unsophisticated, ill-mannered out-of-towner who just happened to be a genius when it came to putting a magazine together. 'Why', he was once asked by a disappointed cartoonist, 'do you reject drawings of mine, and print stuff by that fifth-rate artist Thurber?' 'Third-rate,' replied Ross, thus managing simultaneously to damn and defend his protégé. He dared to ask questions of contributors that other editors might have been afraid or too embarrassed to raise. Once, he wondered why, in a story whose telling had spanned a day and more, no one seemed to have had anything to eat. How plausible was that? Among his many *bêtes noires* were clichés, adverbs, puns, sex (as a subject), sentences that began with an 'and' or a 'but', and the use of French phrases such as *bête noire*.

When Ross died in 1951 at the age of 59, there was no need for a *New Yorker* equivalent of a papal conclave. No white smoke was seen billowing from its headquarters on Manhattan's West 43rd Street. Ross's anointed successor was William Shawn, who had joined the magazine in 1933 and who was as shy, self-effacing and courteous as Ross had been brusque, bellicose and bloody-minded. It was Shawn who decided to devote the best part of an issue to a slightly abridged version of *The Prime of Miss Jean Brodie*, an accolade that had previously been awarded only to John Hersey for his long essay *Hiroshima*, which told the story of six survivors of the atomic bomb dropped on the eponymous city. Shawn – known to everyone outside his family as Mr Shawn – was not an impetuous man. Alastair Reid, Muriel's friend and mine, who was a staff writer on the *New Yorker* for half a century, liked to tell how Shawn was content to hold up the printing presses while he and Alastair debated the merit of a comma over a semicolon. For Alastair, this was a measure of the care Shawn took to get things right; for others, it suggested obsessiveness bordering on psychosis.

From Muriel's point of view Shawn was someone whom she could trust. Unlike so many other men she had encountered, if he made a promise she could be sure he would keep it. He found her an office in the magazine's headquarters which, though small and spartan, was in a much sought after location in the building. To the dismay (and envy) of a number of other more biddable and venerable writers attached to the magazine, she had the battleship-grey walls repainted in a bright colour – why, as she was wont to say, make a dull day even duller? – and brought in her own furnishings to improve the ambience, including an indigo-blue carpet and a turquoise divan. This meant she had a base in New York City and could come and go as she pleased; it was available to her whenever she chose to use it.

In particular, she liked the way Shawn comported himself. He had the mien of a monk. A teetotaller in an era when long liquid lunches were the norm, he was unlikely ever to be seen slumped over a bar in the pose patented by so many of the magazine's cartoonists. He seemed devoid of ego and would resist argument wherever possible. A. J. Liebling once likened him to Mahatma Gandhi. Liebling also suggested he had much in common with Winston Churchill, which is harder to fathom. In the fifty-four years Shawn spent at the *New Yorker* his byline did not once appear in its pages. His many phobias included a fear of automatic elevators, which in a city of skyscrapers was eccentric to say the least. His loyalty to the magazine and its contributors was unbreakable but not always reciprocated. In 1965, when he and the *New Yorker* were subjected to a cruel and malicious parody by Tom Wolfe, Muriel was one of the few writers to swing a baseball bat in his defence. From bitter personal experience, she appreciated that loyalty was precious and that bullies had to be confronted.

Alastair Reid was one of her closest friends in New York. He had begun writing for the *New Yorker* in the early 1950s and for more than half a century was a staff writer, albeit one whose appearances at West 43rd Street were fleeting and irregular. The son of a Church of Scotland minister, he was born in Whithorn, Galloway, in 1926. He died in 2014. Like Muriel, he felt more at ease with his native land when he was no longer living there. His view of Scotland, coloured by his upbringing, was that of a cheerless, monochrome and inward-looking place where the Kirk cast a presbyterian pall that lowered the spirits. After the Second World War, Alastair sought to make his home in warmer and more relaxed places. His many stamp-packed passports were testimony to a life lived on the hoof. He was a wanderer, a cosmopolitan, relentlessly peripatetic, who taught himself Spanish and translated the poems of Jorge Luis Borges and Pablo Neruda, both of whom he befriended, and many others.

In the 1950s, Alastair lived in Deya, Majorca, where he was accepted as part of Robert Graves' extended family. As he

Muriel in the 1960s, no longer a girl of slender means

acknowledged, Graves had found the ideal way to make a living as a writer. 'He often said that he bred show dogs in order to be able to afford a cat. The dogs were prose; the cat was poetry.' It was a lesson Alastair took to heart. Having first made an impact at the *New Yorker* as a poet, he persuaded Shawn to appoint him its Spanish correspondent. He soon extended his brief to Central and South America and became one of the first to recognise the genius of magical realists such as the Colombian Gabriel Garcia Márquez and the Peruvian Mario Vargas Llosa, both of whose fiction he was instrumental in introducing to an English-speaking readership by championing them in the *New Yorker*.

As the only Scots at the *New Yorker* it was inevitable that Muriel and Alastair would become friends. But while they shared some characteristics, they were opposites in others. Alastair was a domestic animal, the kind of person who was content to look after other people's houses for a few weeks while their owners was elsewhere. He liked to cook, and was a dab hand at making soup or mince and tatties, though I did not share his belief that the addition of ginger – which he had farmed in the Dominican Republic – could improve almost any dish. Muriel, on the other hand, was more likely to be a house's owner than its sitter. When Alastair travelled it was with the minimum of luggage. Once, he turned up at my place with all of his belongings stuffed into a plastic carrier bag – something which would have astonished Muriel. He wore clothes that were bought for their convenience rather than their appearance. Mostly, he shopped from catalogues or in stores that catered for backpackers. His favoured trousers and shirts were made from fabrics that kept him warm in winter and cool in summer, and which could be washed and dried overnight. Muriel, who did not subscribe to the view that 'Levi's' was a designer label, said he was 'the second-worst-dressed man in New York', prompting me to wonder who was the worst. While she was oblivious to life's practicalities, Alastair gave the impression that were he to be marooned on a desert island he would not just survive but thrive. Once, Muriel told him she had a special guest coming to dinner and was at a loss, given her lack of expertise in the kitchen, how best to cater for him. Alastair suggested she contact the Carnegie Deli, which would deliver food of restaurant-quality to her door. Who, he asked, by the by, was her guest? 'Auden,' she replied. As ever with Muriel the experience was squirrelled away for future use. In her novel, *Reality and Dreams*, published in 1996, Auden in his 'shabby clothes' makes a fleeting appearance: 'He liked to spend his money on food. Wystan gave good dinners. I remember in the sixties when he lived in Manhattan in a near-slum in St Mark's Place what fine food he would sit one down to. At least, his

step into the breach. It took me but a few seconds to say yes. She was 82 and though beset by various maladies she had recently completed *Aiding and Abetting*, her novel about the disappearance of Lord Lucan. The trip would be a reward for hard graft. Penny drove Muriel from Tuscany to London where we met at Durrants Hotel, Marylebone, their usual haunt in the capital. The *New Yorker* had arranged for a car to pick us up and take us to Heathrow on the morning of departure. There, Muriel was transferred to a wheelchair. As one of the Virgin airline staff wheeled her on to the plane he remarked that she could look forward to a good flight. 'Why's that?' asked Muriel. 'Because my boss is on board,' he said. As we took our first-class seats I glanced across the aisle and saw, surrounded by a twitter of cabin crew, Richard Branson. When I told Muriel, she said: 'Let's wait until we're airborne and then we'll ask him over for a drink.' Which I did. He was charmed and the two of them sat and chatted over a glass of champagne for an hour or so. As we disembarked he took me to one side and whispered that he had just heard that Lord Lucan had been found, apparently somewhere in Africa. What, he wondered, might the impact be on Muriel's book? Would she have to rewrite it? The simple answer was I hadn't a clue but while I tried to digest the information Branson said: 'I was only joking!'

The *New Yorker* had booked us adjacent rooms at Morgans on Madison Avenue, 'a new and extremely fine hotel near the Pierpont Morgan Library'. As we drew up in the limo Muriel said, 'Please be sure and tip the driver handsomely.' Later, she inquired if I had done as she had requested and I said I hadn't, simply because he would be available to chauffeur us wherever and whenever we wanted during our stay. There would be plenty of opportunities to remunerate him properly in the days ahead. The hotel was indeed new, so new you could smell it. It was also inadequately illuminated, which would have been fine if one were a coal miner and wearing a headlamp. As Muriel followed a flunkey down a bleak corridor I repeated Dr Johnson's remark to James Boswell as the pair made their way through the odiferous murk of mid-eighteenth century Edinburgh: 'I smell you in the dark!' Muriel replied that it wasn't the worst thing that had been said about her.

The dismal lighting notwithstanding, the Morgan lived up to its billing. In the mornings Muriel breakfasted in bed, and read and wrote. She had a poem 'on the go', as she always did, and there was a play percolating in her head. One day, she asked if I could stick around while she was interviewed by a writer from *Talk*, a relatively new publication founded by Tina Brown, former editor of the *New Yorker*. I said I would be happy to meet the person who was interviewing her but that I would then leave the pair of them to get on with it in private. Did she know who the interviewer was? 'Paul Theroux,' she said, pronouncing his name as if she had never come across it before. Afterwards I asked her how the encounter had gone. She said that she had liked Theroux and in many respects the interview was perfect for the simple reason that he had talked mainly about himself and had hardly directed a question at her.

On another day, close to lunchtime, Muriel said she would like to visit the Metropolitan Museum of Art. There was a queue which we joined, Muriel wheelchair-bound. Suddenly, there appeared at our side a harassed-looking woman who asked: 'Are you Muriel Spark?' She had been informed of our arrival by the *New Yorker*, which seemed to have a CIA-like ability to keep tabs on our movements. The woman, who was on the Met's staff, said she was at our disposal for as long as was required and would like nothing more than to give us a conducted tour of the museum's many treasures. Was there anything in particular Muriel would like to see? 'Oh, the shop,' said Muriel, 'then the restaurant.' The tombs of the pharaohs and a villa that had been removed from the ruins of Pompeii could wait. At the shop she bought an Egyptian-style necklace for Rene, in compensation for me being borrowed by her for the trip.

Later that afternoon I told Muriel I needed to find somewhere which could quickly alter the sleeves on a few shirts I had bought at Brooks Brothers. I had identified what looked like a suitable establishment a block away from the Morgan that was run by a Chinese family. Muriel said she would have to witness this and sat shaking with laughter while I tried to explain what was required to a Chinese woman holding a measuring tape between her teeth. As we left the shop, Muriel said she would not be surprised if my long-sleeved shirts were altered into short-sleeved ones, so confusing were my pathetic attempts at communication.

Throughout our stay in New York Muriel seemed as carefree as I imagined she had been when she first arrived there in 1961, fascinated by everything and everyone. It was easy to forget that she was in her ninth decade and in constant pain. I couldn't help but compare her with the elderly cast of *Memento Mori*. 'How primitive life becomes in old age,' thinks one of them, 'when one may be surrounded by familiar comforts and yet more vulnerable to the action of nature than any young explorer at the Pole.' Muriel's approach to ageing – and the infirmity that was its inevitable accompaniment – seemed to be to ignore it wherever possible. To her, illness was an inconvenience which needed to be dealt with quickly, like a leaky roof or a squeaky hinge. Being in New York had an energising effect on her; it was as if she had taken a performance-enhancing drug. Every day was there to be seized. Hers was a notebook that was never closed. She was always watching, listening, accumulating, questioning. The past was past; what mattered was the present and the future.

Towards the end of our stay we went to lunch in Little Italy. The restaurant was more or less empty, save for a man of pensionable age endeavouring to impress his much younger female accessory. Muriel surmised that she was his mistress and he was her sugar daddy. She put a finger to her lips and tuned her antennae to their conversation. The pair studied the menu with the intensity of archaeologists poring over one of the Dead Sea Scrolls. The woman, it appeared, could find nothing on it that was to her liking. With a snap of his fingers, the man summoned a waiter, who stood rigidly by the table like one of the Swiss guards on parade at the Vatican. From what Muriel could make out the sugar daddy was describing in excruciating detail a dish that his companion would like to eat but which for some reason was not on the menu. The waiter listened impassively. His demeanour was that of someone who has seen and heard it all before and who is not of the school that believes the customer is always right. The diner, oblivious to the fuss he was causing, continued to outline the dish his companion would like to have served. He exuded authority; he was the kind of man who was used to getting what he wanted. Round his neck was a gold chain of mayoral heft. His suit was shiny, his patent shoes even shinier. His shirt was at least a collar size too small and wiry hair spilled out from his chest like weeds through a crack in a pavement. He enjoyed the sound of his own voice. When he had finished giving orders, he handed the waiter the menu and turned to the young woman, whose face was a picture of impassivity. The waiter did not move. The man looked up, as if to say, 'What are you hovering for, man, get on with it, we're hungry, chop-chop.' The waiter explained to him that a menu contains what a restaurant has to offer. 'It is not a blank sheet of paper on which you can draw up your own menu. Now I would like you to leave.' The man looked at the woman, who studied the floor. 'Please, you must leave now,' said the waiter, brooking no further exchange. As the man put on his coat and helped the woman into hers, he looked what he was: deflated, defeated, humiliated. Muriel relished the performance much more than the faux Italian food that followed. What might otherwise have been a lunch to forget had been transformed into a dramatic performance worthy of Broadway.

Muriel talked often and fondly of the days when she had an office at the *New Yorker*. Reading accounts by people who knew her then one senses how different she was from other writers and, to a degree, other women. Brendan Gill, the magazine's chief gossipmonger, told whoever had ears that, having been 'positively obese' and a dreary bookworm, she had become a chic and glamorous diva. Her sometime secretary, Janet Groth, has written in her 2012 memoir, *The Receptionist*, how Muriel – 'my fairy godmother' – managed simultaneously to be sociable and isolated, turning down many more invitations than she accepted. At an office party, Groth recalled, she arrived with 'a very young and handsome blond – a gent from her agent's office, I was given to understand. She looked beautiful in a strapless yellow chiffon dress accessorised with silver stiletto slippers and a rhinestone brooch centred on its bosom. She sported some David Webb bracelets on her slender arms, and her hair was freshly done in a reddish-blond bouffant. She made a typically generous contribution to the proceedings, her escort leaving at least a jeroboam of Dom Pérignon at the paper-draped bar.'

One evening, when we were on our way to dinner with Georges and Anne Borchardt, Muriel's literary agents, she asked the chauffeur to drive past the one-bedroom apartment at Perry Street and Seventh Avenue in the West Village which she had bought in the late 1980s as an investment. It was part of a modern block of six storeys. We couldn't go in, she said, because it was let. She just wanted to make sure it was still standing. We also passed the Beaux Arts Hotel where she had lived in the 1960s. She had written an article about it for *Nest*, a short-lived lifestyle magazine, which she sent to me after we returned to Europe. It was an eccentric publication. It included pieces about the final resting place of Napoleon's penis, for example, and the room of a 40-year-old diaper lover.

By those standards, Muriel's contribution bordered on the banal. In the Beaux Arts Hotel, she recalled, she had 'virtually' two rooms, and a galley kitchen with a gas stove. The management allowed tenants to choose their own decor, which they could change every six months if what they had originally chosen was not to their liking. Muriel's first choices were mustard wall-to-wall carpeting with turquoise-blue upholstery, white walls and white curtains with large yellow flowers. 'Maybe', she acknowledged, 'this sounds awful but it looked like a dream.' She had a maid who brought eight clean towels a day, four in the morning, four at night. The bed linen was changed every day, and meals – prepared by the restaurant on the ground floor – could be wheeled in at any hour of the day or night. Bliss it was to be a resident of the Beaux Arts. Muriel had never before basked in such luxury. For all of this 'plus a few trimmings' she paid a basic $450 a month.

On our visit, the *New Yorker* made few demands of her. There was a lunch with its editor David Remnick and the writer Stephen Schiff, who had profiled her for the magazine a number of years previously. Schiff had perceptively identified God as the main character in her fiction, though He is never portrayed on the page. 'One might say', he'd noted, 'that the way she worships God is by trying to see things from his point of view.' In tandem with Julian Barnes, she was asked to read a story to an audience in a small theatre. She chose 'A Hundred and Eleven Years Without a Chauffeur', which was soon to appear in the *New Yorker*. In it, at the request of her biographer, a famous female writer goes in search of family photographs, some of which she realises have gone missing. It was an idea that perhaps had its origins in Muriel's recent appointment of her official biographer, Martin Stannard.

After the reading and a question and answer session there was a drinks party at the Gramercy Park apartment of Bill Buford, the *New Yorker*'s then fiction editor. Muriel and I sat with Julian at the kitchen table while in another room Salman Rushdie chatted to Alice Munro. Next to Muriel was an empty chair which a man asked if he might take; he was David Hockney. On another evening there was the *New Yorker*'s 75th anniversary celebration at the Bryant Park Grill. Alastair Reid was reunited with Muriel at the Morgan and travelled with us to the event. Muriel spent a couple of hours meeting old friends and being introduced to new ones. As things began to swing, she said it was time for us to make our excuses and leave. When I pointed out that we had only been there for a short while, she said: 'We've done our duty.' She was not tired, simply ready to move on. She asked if the chauffeur might be able to recommend somewhere good to eat. All that was required was steak and salad and a glass of red wine. 'Leave it to me,' said the chauffeur. Half an hour later we were outside a swanky restaurant and escorted via a red carpet by the maître d' to a banquette where, already poured and waiting for us, were two large glasses of a good Chianti.

Muriel returned to San Giovanni in high spirits despite the fact that over the course of our visit she had broken two toes and a rib, and had a slight fever and higher blood pressure. It was all due to what Penny described as New York's mania for 'womb-lighting'. It was the beginning of a bout of very bad luck. First, in June, the house was struck by lightning. 'Gone were the phones,' wrote Muriel to me, 'water-pump, air-conditioner, three roofs. The bell-tower fell into my bathroom at 2 a.m. Monday last. I happened not to be there but got a burnt lip. Penelope has been getting temporary faxes and phones and keeping her head . . . We will be here last week of July and last three weeks of August. The stars contend with us.'

A few weeks later Penny sent an update:

We are recovering in that the church roof has been covered with tin and Muriel's bathroom with plastic. This has been called work of '*somma urgenza*'. No more work is allowed to be done until the architect has made a *progetto* and the Town Hall and the dreaded Fine Arts bureaucrats have approved the plan. The builders have put up huge scaffolding inside and out. Muriel is still without her bathroom and forbidden her bedroom on stormy nights (in case the other half of the bell-tower collapses). All this is fairly unsatisfactory to us who live here, but we may have to wait 'months' before the builders can move again. Meanwhile the dreaded end of summer storms will strike . . .

We drive off on Sunday with the predicted 18 million Italians going on holiday . . . The accidents on the roads are horrific, but we will grit our little British teeth and thrust out our winning little chins. This way we should reach Chambery in the Savoie on Sunday night, the peaceful Château Barive near Laon on Monday and Cambridge on Tuesday. There we will confront those strange species called the British Council and their flock of foreign and British writers: Christopher Fry, David Lodge, Melvyn Bragg, Doris Lessing, et al.

Building work progressed slowly. In October, the roof was still unfixed and water dripped monotonously into bowls. One night thunder struck at 2 a.m. and then again at 4 a.m. and Penny had to rush around with a torch switching off all appliances, lest they be rendered useless. They were due soon to set off for London. 'Muriel,' wrote Penny, 'is to receive a Golden Plate at the banquet at Hampton Court. I hope it won't have anyone's head on it.' Meanwhile the house continued to leak like a colander, and Muriel could be seen 'wading disconsolately into her bathroom (which she is not allowed to enter) in her waders, sou'wester and wind-cheater'.

Then, in November, on their way to London, Muriel got a call on her mobile phone. There had been a serious break-in at San Giovanni. There was no option but to turn round immediately. Penny drove for eleven hours with barely a stop. The thieves had stolen paintings, sculptures and many items of personal and sentimental value, including Muriel's collection of pens. Only the books were left untouched. Patrizia, the maid, was in a state of hysteria. 'I feel more for Penelope's things as they are her work and irreplaceable,' Muriel told me. 'Mine are more just *stuff*... We are amazed that they took the refrigerator too, daintily piling the contents on the kitchen table.' The walls were empty, save for a few picture hooks which merely added to the gloom. The house was littered with white grapes, an indication of how long the thieves had been able to spend in it.

Muriel and Penny longed to go away but couldn't because the builders were at last working on the roof. The thieves, it seemed, must have known that the house was unoccupied. They had spent a lot of effort unnecessarily breaking down doors when they could easily have got in through windows. 'We can't help thinking', surmised Penny, 'the criminals are almost known to us, and *near*.' She and Muriel had their suspicions as to who was responsible but had no proof. Almost every lock had been sawn through and an armchair had been left in a field, presumably because someone had seen what was going on and had raised the alarm. 'All this between you and me (and the gatepost),' wrote Penny. 'Muriel and I both lost many irreplaceable things, alas. But then you can't take them with you ... My sister said "Put on the music loud and scream!" Unfortunately they took the newly-mended, lightning-struck stereo ...'

Muriel, meanwhile, in the midst of all this turmoil, had turned sleuth. Writing on the eve of the New Year, she pondered: 'Who done it?', adding 'we have various theories worthy of Agatha Christie and so far no results'. Thus ended what she designated an 'anno orribile'.

Muriel's desk at San Giovanni

6

A QUESTION OF JEWISHNESS

❡

There's always more to it than Jew, Gentile, half-Jew, half-Gentile.
There's the human soul, the individual. Not 'Jew, Gentile' as one
might say 'autumn, winter'. Something unique and unrepeatable.

THE MANDELBAUM GATE

In Tuscany, as the year draws to a close, it rains often and thunderously to the accompaniment of operatic flashes of lightning. Once the olives have been safely harvested the countryside grows sombre and somnambulant. In that regard, it is reminiscent of the Scottish borders with its dun colours, moss-covered drystane dykes and isolated farms; all that's missing is the bleating of sheep and the keening cry of a solitary curlew. Late autumn was always a good time to visit Muriel and Penny though it must be said that San Giovanni was not the warmest of houses. The rooms were mostly large and dark, and the ancient radiators struggled to maintain the temperature above freezing. The kitchen, with its soot-smeared, wardrobe-sized hearth, was the cosiest of the twenty or so rooms. Here we three would sit for hours on end as afternoon drifted towards evening. The fire was fed with wood gathered from the nearby fields and forest, which was the domain of wild boar. One December I woke to the sound of boughs cracking under the weight of snow which was lying thick and deep. This was the Val di Chiana as I had never seen it before. All was white save for the leaden sky from which yet more snow threatened to fall. After a few hours the stillness was broken by the sound of a municipal snow plough grinding up the hill towards Civitella. At Penny's behest, I asked the man in charge if he would also clear San Giovanni's driveway, which he agreed readily to do. In so doing, however, he managed in his enthusiasm to remove a substantial layer of top soil, which meant that when the snow melted what had formerly been firm ground on which to park a car was now an inescapable quagmire.

Those were cheery, intimate occasions, with no imperative, and sometimes not even the possibility, to leave the policies. As dusk fell wine bottles replaced coffee pots, and Muriel, having stopped work for the day, could relax and unwind. How well I remember the look of concern on her face when, in the midst of a blizzard, Penny announced that we had just opened the last bottle of wine in the house. Muriel was not alone in her relief when Penny assured us that a plentiful supply remained in a cellar accessible from the outside. In the spirit of altruistic Captain Oates of the Antarctic, I volunteered to don a coat and fetch fresh supplies. Unlike him, I promised to make a speedy return.

As she advanced into her eighties, Muriel's health continued to cause concern. In his biography, published in 2009, three years after her death, Martin Stannard indexes a litany of ailments, a number of which – appendectomy, hysterectomy, hernia, sundry fractures, hip replacements, cataracts, cancer – caused extreme pain and discomfort and were severely debilitating. Muriel's reaction was to seek panaceas which would allow her to return to her desk as quickly as possible. She had a pharmacist's knowledge of drugs and was always prepared to try a new and unproven one if she thought it would make her feel any better. On Boxing Day 1998, for instance, she wrote to tell me of 'a miracle drug' called Artrosilene which a trustworthy local nurse called Marzi injected into her every day. 'It's amazing,' she wrote. 'If . . . you have arthritis I can recommend it.' How efficacious it proved was difficult to assess. Meanwhile, Muriel was still dealing with the fallout from various hip replacement operations, including one in an Italian hospital which involved sawing a femur in half; it was done while she still semi-conscious and she had been able to observe it as it happened. She loved to tell, too, of a letter she had received from an English surgeon – one of whose patients had been the Queen Mother – who had performed yet another hip operation on her, informing her that, subsequently, he had had an operation which had transformed him from a man into a woman. Would this put Muriel off using him, or her, again? She said that she would need to give the idea very careful consideration. Certainly, she did not want to be put under sedation as a woman and wake up a few hours later to discover she was of another gender. But she did concede that it was an intriguing premise on which to build a novel. 'I'll have to think about that,' she mused.

Though she may have been a physical wreck, Muriel was indubitably mentally alert, unlike her friend, Iris Murdoch, who died in 1999 after suffering from Alzheimer's. Muriel was incensed by the several memoirs written during Iris's lifetime by her husband, John Bayley, in which he described in unsparing detail Iris's descent into dementia. To Muriel, it was a betrayal of trust, a gross and callous act of disloyalty. She did not believe, as some others did, that it was written out of grief and could be interpreted as a valedictory love letter. This was not Muriel's reading of those books. On the contrary, she felt they were exploitative and mercenary and self-serving. So incensed was she at the publicising of Iris's degeneration that, together with her friend Doris Lessing, she wrote a letter to *The Times* expressing her outrage. It was never sent. On 27 February 1999, shortly after Iris's death, Muriel wrote to Doris: 'It was a good thing that Iris was spared further suffering. For some reason or other – it is really inexplicable – John Bayley gives me the creeps. He once said to me, "You're a dear little thing but you don't really believe all that rubbish about the Church, do you?" (As if I'd say it if I didn't.) I hated that "dear little thing" – f**k him.' A few months later, in the summer of 1999, Muriel was given an honorary degree by Oxford University and she asked if I would like to join Penny and her at the ceremony. That evening a dinner was held in her honour to which, to her dismay, Bayley was invited. At her insistence he was placed at the opposite end of the table from where she was sitting. In fact, he was so far away she could barely see him. It was the best revenge she could exact on Iris's behalf.

Alan Taylor with Muriel in Oxford, 1999, when she received an honorary degree

What blighted Muriel's final decade, however, was her relationship with her son, Robin, the very mention of whose name could cast a cloud over the brightest gathering. It got to the point where she preferred not to talk about him, and she did her best to cast him from her mind. That was easier said than done. Few months went by when their 'feud', as many newspapers labelled it, did not resurface. It was like another pernicious ailment for which there was not even a quack cure. In the media she was frequently portrayed as the guilty party, a neglectful mother who had forsaken her only child, as if she had left him on a doorstep, while she had pursued fame and fortune regardless of his welfare. It did not help that when interviewed she gave unguarded replies. Asked, for example, about Robin's paintings – his themes were invariably associated with his Jewishness and obsession with Judaism – she did not take the diplomatic option of staying silent, once telling the *Telegraph*: 'He always wanted me to say [his paintings] were good but I didn't think they were. Art is important to me and I wasn't going to commit perjury . . . If he wants to be a victim, he can be a victim.'

To anyone who was unfamiliar with the history of their relationship, it was easy to draw the conclusion that it was Robin who was wronged and that it was Muriel who was responsible for the rupture. It was much more complicated than that. Happiness was not a state to which Muriel aspired. She thought it overrated and believed the quest for it was doomed to result in disappointment and worse. For what could you do with happiness once you felt you had found it? Hang on to it? Aspire to be even more happy? All she could do was follow the path laid out by Cardinal Newman – her mentor in so many matters – who believed that by working hard and living well you might achieve contentment. But the situation with Robin precluded any prolonged sense of that. It was something she had to learn to live with or do her best to ignore. Nothing that she could say or do, it seemed, could repair the hurt that had been caused on both sides. Words that might have been better left unsaid had been said and could not be retracted. The only advice I could give her was in future to decline all requests for interviews. Even saying 'no comment' suggested she had something to hide. If, in the course of meeting her obligations to her publishers, she felt she had to speak to the media she should refuse to entertain questions about the relationship between her and her only offspring. For as she would readily acknowledge, she was not naturally maternal. 'I don't think I was an ideal mother', she said, 'but I know that I did the best I could and that he didn't suffer at all.'

Cast as the villain in a plot, she of all people must have appreciated the irony of her abusive and mentally unstable ex-husband being given the role of hero according to her own son's unreliable testimony. This was recorded by Robin in an article published in 1999 in the *Edinburgh Star*, the voice of the local Jewish community. It was remarkable for its unstinting praise of Sydney Oswald Spark and the solitary passing mention it made of Muriel who, though she had been denied custody of Robin in South Africa, ensured that his upbringing was as happy as it could be in the circumstances. It was she who paid for her mother and father to look after him, ensuring he wanted for nothing. His father, meanwhile, was at best feckless and at worst certifiable, a danger to himself and others. For a brief period, SOS had lived with Muriel's parents who soon realised it was an arrangement that could not continue. In 1947, when Robin was nine, his father was suspended from his teaching job for whacking a pupil with a leather strap known as a tawse. Though the use of the 'belt' as it was called was common in Scottish schools at that period, it was not permissible to hit a boy on the face. Throughout this time, Sydney Spark did everything he could to stop Robin joining Muriel in London where she was trying to make ends meet.

None of this features in the article 'Life with the Cambergs'. Instead, Robin produced a varnished portrait of his upbringing with his maternal grandparents, with whom life was apparently never dull. 'The Cambergs', he wrote, 'were warm, friendly, outgoing people who attracted like-minded people of different faiths and persuasions. My own tolerance and love of different peoples is largely due to my having taken on board their philosophy of life.' His tolerance did not extend to his mother, who seemed barely to be on his radar. Instead, he preferred to dwell on his bar mitzvah and subsequent celebrations at the Balmoral Restaurant in Princes Street, all paid for by Muriel, who declined to attend the event to avoid any clash with her former husband. Robin wrote, too, about the Russian roots of his father, who apparently was 'a brilliant scholar' who would have liked to pursue a career in medicine but was thwarted because there were no means to pay for it. Conspicuous by its absence is any mention of Sydney Spark's mental instability, and his erratic, violent conduct and confinement in a lunatic asylum. Rather than mention these unfortunate facts, or his illustrious mother, Robin wrote: 'Among my dearest possessions is the samovar my grandfather Samuel Spark brought with him from his home in Lithuania. It has pride of place by my lounge fireside.'

Muriel with her son Robin in Rhodesia, c.1942. Custody of the child was awarded to her husband

Presented as a genial exercise in nostalgia, 'Life with the Cambergs' is in truth a disingenuous, misleading piece of work, designed to serve its author's own ends. So pleased with it was Robin, and so determined it should have a life beyond the publication in which it first appeared, that in 2013 he had it reprinted as a pamphlet. Such an act could only serve to deepen the rift between son and mother. There can be little doubt it was calculated to do just that. When Muriel read it, having probably been sent it by the author, she was disgusted. Robin, she believed, had been brainwashed by his father who, while she was busy elsewhere making a living, had turned her son, Iago-like, against her. Sydney's obsessiveness, his paranoia, his victimhood, was the inheritance he passed on to his son. With their shared sense of hurt, father and son were disturbingly alike.

At what point did Muriel's relationship with Robin begin to sour? It is difficult to give an exact date. As they grew older their respective positions became more entrenched. The less they saw of each other, the further apart they grew. There were letters and phone calls and expressions of love, exchanges of gifts and a common and abiding interest in cats but one also had the sense that they did not feel easy in one another's company. Both Muriel and Penny invited Robin to visit them at San Giovanni but he never took up the offer. Throughout his life it seemed to her that he did not want to settle down long enough in a job to make a proper go of it. Leaving school when he was sixteen, he worked for a while in a jeweller's shop then flirted with the antiques trade before joining the civil service. Latterly he pursued a career as an artist while earning a regular income as a junior employee in the National Galleries of Scotland. In all of these enthusiasms Muriel humoured and encouraged him while quietly biting her tongue. After all, he was her son.

There were occasions when she must have felt that the relationship was never going to improve. One such was the death in 1962 of her father, when Robin was 24 and she was 44. In her essay 'What Images Return', mentioned in an earlier chapter, she wrote in its opening sentence that she was 'obliged' to spend some weeks in the North British Hotel while Bertie Camberg's illness ran its inevitable course. The word 'obliged' is telling. I had always assumed that she had decided to book into the hotel rather than the family home because there was no room for her there. The more likely reason was, as Penny once suggested to me, that Robin told Muriel bluntly to 'get out', which, not wishing to further upset her mother, she duly did. Over the course of the years, there were several similar emotionally draining incidents. By far the most damaging in the long term, however, was their fundamental disagreement over whether Muriel was wholly Jewish.

The story is told in a series of letters between Muriel and Robin that are lodged in the National Library of Scotland. In the early exchanges they contain the kind of material that one might expect to find in the correspondence between a mother and her son. Robin is referred to as 'dearest Rob', 'my handsome boy', on whom a constellation of kisses is bestowed. Muriel encouraged him to find a girlfriend, keep painting, sent him cheques ('I made it £110 as it is better than £100, isn't it?') and kept him abreast of her news. She told him of her meeting the Queen Mother ('who expressed admiration for my books, which she reads') and offered advice of the kind often to be found in her novels: 'Appearances count a great deal . . . Why be middle-aged before you're young? You should look like the son of a successful mother any way without being showy (as you never are) . . . I feel more vigorous and confident in every way when I wear my jazzy clothes instead of all that old ladies' crap. It has a psychological effect when you go around looking 100% in the casual new styles.'

Mostly, she was on the receiving end of Robin's woes but now and then she offloaded some of her own. 'I'm not a man – not anyone's husband, father or son – but a woman, after all, and a self-supporting one with an aged mother to provide for and provide for decently,' she wrote in February 1966. 'I can't take on any more burdens – whether financial or merely in correspondence & discussion. Don't you agree? You know, darling, I rarely go into *my* problems and responsibilities, and the only reason I'm telling you this is to enable you to understand my prudence in keeping my whereabouts & movement private.' Trips home were clearly a trial. She once told Robin that, if she were to visit, 'I would have to be absolutely sure there would be no more unpleasantness and abuse. Some people enjoy it, I don't. I know you'll appreciate my frankness, and if I may say so, many people around you have treated their own families very badly, and have been on the grabbing side – and yet presume to criticise me who have [sic] treated my family well, even although I am a woman without a provider. I think you have sometimes been influenced by such people.'

Many months would go by when Muriel had no communication from Robin. His silence felt like a reproof. Then, at the beginning of 1981, he wrote out of the blue to inform her of his research into the family's genealogy, and of his insistence that she must be wholly Jewish because, according to what he had found out, her female forebears had been Jews. It was the first shot in a war

of words in which there would be no ceasefire until both of
the duellists were dead. The second was a letter from Muriel,
dated 10 February, 1981, in which she sought gently but firmly
to correct Robin's rewriting of her past:

> My maternal grandmother Adelaide was a ½ Jew from
> her father's side, an Abrams. Her mother was a gentile.
> I remember an old Hen called Mrs Lipitz rubbing this in
> to my father, much to my mother's embarrassment, but
> my Dad said he didn't care a damn . . . Anyway, Adelaide
> was married in Watford Parish Church to Thomas Uzzell.
> All these things, including Adelaide's mother's name are
> on the record in London and in Watford. I could never
> be bothered to dig into it all, but the experts and scholars
> might well do so after my death.
>
> Facts are facts and should be recorded objectively
> as such and not distorted, but it's what you do with your
> life that counts – that's my philosophy. My grandmother
> Adelaide was a great card, and I've written about her in
> my piece 'The Gentile Jewesses' which of course is straight
> true fact. My brother Phil says there's a memorial to
> her in Watford churchyard where my grandfather Tom
> Uzzell lies. My own good Jewish blood comes from the
> Camberg side. They also came later in the 19th century
> to Edinburgh. My father was born in Edinburgh, went to
> Warrender Park School, ran away to sea at 14, was hauled
> back from Kirkwall and put as an apprentice to Bertram's
> Motor Works.

Had Robin read the piece to which Muriel refers – as he must
surely have done – he will have seen, set out as plainly as

possible, what his mother's position was. It was impossible, she recognised, 'to separate' the Jewess within her from the Gentile. In her mind, the two coexisted in harmony, 'uncomplainingly amongst one's own bones'. Was she a Gentile? Or a Jewess? 'Both and neither. What am I? I am what I am.' It would appear that, for his part, Robin could not cope with such ambiguity. He craved certainty. To him, a person must be one thing or the other. There was no middle ground, no shade of grey, no debateable land. His was a monochrome world, in which one must be either Jew or Gentile. Consequently, he had no sympathy, or empathy, with his mother's point of view. So, rather than let a sleeping dog lie, he allowed a couple of months to go by, then he replied to Muriel's letter in a patronising tone that seemed hellbent on provocation:

The contents of your letter of 10 February cause me some concern. You should know that if your maternal grandmother . . . was a gentile then under Jewish law all issue are declared gentiles, unless she converted according the rights of Judaism and sanctioned by Beth Din. If your grandmother's mother became a proselyte then all issue would be Jews. There is no [such] term in Judaism as a ½ Jew . . .

Had your great-grandmother in question been or married a gentile then according to the Beth Din – the Jewish official religious court – all children between her and a Jew would have been regarded as gentiles. One 'inherits' one's Judaism or right to be a Jew from one's mother who would have to be a Jewess or a convert to Judaism.

I have a copy of an article from, I think, the *New York Times* of May 20, 1979 by Victoria Glendinning which says that you were '. . . brought up in Scotland as a Presbyterian

. . .' I find this very distressing and unlikely in view of your parents' Orthodox Jewish Wedding and their membership all their lives in Edinburgh of the Hebrew Congregation and your brother's Jewish religious education and Barmitzvah in this city. And I would like to think that was not your quote or if so a mis-quote. Most of us follow the religion, if any, of our forebears, and this presumably is what Gran and Granpa must have decided.

In her reply, dated 2 May, Muriel finally lost patience with Robin. He had no business, she said, trying to tell her about her upbringing. He hadn't been there; she had. Her mother and father were not at all orthodox. Apart from anything else, they loved bacon and eggs and pork and pig's trotters, about which she thought she might one day write. Her father, she added, was a fine man who though he 'put himself down' as Jew was not of the orthodox tendency. Moreover, her own education at Gillespie's was 'entirely Presbyterian'. Unlike other Jewish girls she was given Bible lessons. When she got married in Rhodesia it was in a magistrate's office, not a synagogue. Robin, meanwhile, was medically not religiously circumcised.

> These are facts. My Watford grandmother's mother *was* a gentile. My mother's marriage in Stepney Synagogue must have been either a nominal conversion or officiated over by a less strict Rabbi, as is well known existed even in those days.
>
> It doesn't matter a damn what you are but you have to get your arithmetic and facts straight. It amazes me when you say that all this causes you 'some concern'. What concern? You aren't going to be judged for good or

evil by what you are, but by what you do. Anyway, you aren't a young girl and you aren't a child. If you don't like FACTS you still have to accept them.

That's all I have to say on the subject and for your own good I do suggest you don't question other people's statements unless you're quite sure of them, with the evidence. I really fail to see what you're driving at half the time. *Nobody* is saying you are not a Jew, or that I have no Jewish origins. You can be whatever you like. My brother Philip would agree, I know. But there's no use writing to me with all that pompous bureaucratic religiosity as if you were John Knox in drag.

One can only imagine the effect of this letter on Robin who, it should be remembered, at the time of its receipt, was sixty years old. Its severity, however, was born out of decades of frustration. Muriel had been prodded once too often and she was in no mood to sugar her sentiments. She had tried to reason with Robin but it was hopeless. He wouldn't listen, nor would he take a hint. He replied more or less immediately. This time, however, his letter was typed rather than hand written, as if to emphasise its formality. If there had been any possibility of a rapprochement this ensured that there could be none:

> If what you say about the female line in your family were true, and consequently your parents' Jewish marriage certificate was obtained under false pretences then by virtue of this neither your brother nor yourself would be recognised by any orthodox Jewish Community in the World.
>
> I know you to be a highly intelligent lady; and I am aware that although I have explained much in detail I doubt

whether you have learned anything new of any great substance from me. You know the score. I would have, therefore, some serious misgivings about the integrity of some of your statements with regard to the female line, and it would seem that the salient points you mention are based more on notional desire on your part than fact . . .

I must now point out to you that I cannot correspond with you further. I am sorry, but I will be unable to see you on your visit to Edinburgh next month. I do hope, however, you keep well and have a pleasant sojourn here with your friends.

For over a year and a half after this letter was written there was little or no communication between mother and son. Muriel did continue to send Robin cheques which, it transpired, he did not care to cash. Finally, in December, 1982, he returned three cheques totalling £700. 'It must be obvious', he wrote, 'that I do not want your gifts, and I would be grateful if you would stop phoning me.' An impasse had been reached that would prove impossible to breach. Like a dormant volcano the 'feud' threatened periodically to erupt and spill over into the pages of the newspapers. Philip, Muriel's brother, who was living in San Diego, California, took her side and confirmed her story. In April 1992, Robin received a phone call from him. 'What are you doing upsetting your mother?' asked Philip. 'I am going to get someone to tear you apart. You little bastard.' Whereupon Robin replaced the receiver and wrote an account of what had happened which he later deposited in the National Library of Scotland.

Some six years later, in March 1998, when I was deputy editor of the *Scotsman*, I was shown a letter sent to the paper by Robin, in which he insisted that he had not instigated the controversy regarding his mother's Jewish origins. Muriel, he asserted, without offering any proof, had been born to a Jewish mother, ergo she must be a Jew. He did concede that her religion is 'her own business, and no-one else's', though several of his letters to her suggest the opposite. He went on: 'Needless to say, it would be embarrassing for me now to find that my grandmother was not Jewish on her mother's side, as has been asserted, since this would mean that I myself am not Jewish according to Orthodox law. But it would not be a disaster for me, since I have been reliably informed by the Jewish authorities that my position could quite easily be regularised.'

On receiving a copy of this letter from me, Muriel's response was typically Sparkian: she challenged Robin to take a DNA test in order to 'prove his affiliation'. It was a novel twist in a narrative that was becoming increasingly bizarre. Nothing, though, could cap what happened a few months later when 'a suspect package', sent by Philip, was delivered to Robin at the family home in Bruntsfield. Fearful that it might contain the wherewithal to blow him to kingdom come he called the police who in turn summoned a bomb disposal squad. Numerous flats in the area were evacuated and roads were cordoned off. Comparison with Belfast during The Troubles was made. The *Daily Record* thought the incident of sufficient importance to devote a page to it. It transpired that the package contained nothing more life-endangering than a novelty gift. 'It was more likely to make you laugh than kill you,' said a police source. As a commentary on the whole sad and unnecessary affair it really said it all.

Muriel at the Edinburgh Book Festival in 2004. 'All Edinburgh', the *Guardian* reported, 'had been fighting tooth-and-claw for a seat'

7
THROUGH THIS EVENING AND INTO TONIGHT

*'Do you find,' said Rowland to Chris, 'that at a certain point your
characters are taking over and living a life of their own?' 'I don't
know what you mean,' Chris said.*

THE FINISHING SCHOOL

*L*oitering With Intent has long been one of my favourites of
Muriel's novels. Published in 1981, when she was sixty-
three, it features a young woman called Fleur Talbot who, when
we first meet her, is sitting in an old graveyard in Kensington
writing a poem. The year is 1950, the date 30 June. At that time,
and in that place, Muriel, like her budding heroine, was on the
cusp of realising herself, of emerging from poverty and giving
wing to her own extraordinary talent.

Two literary shades haunt *Loitering With Intent*. One is
the *Apologia* of Cardinal Newman. The other is Benvenuto
Cellini's *Vita*, from which Muriel quotes on several occasions. It
was the reprobate goldsmith of the Renaissance who declared
that all men 'of whatsoever quality they be' should once they
have passed the age of forty attempt 'to describe their life with
their own hand'. Cellini is Fleur's 'beloved'. She likes everything
about him, good and bad, and is willing to overlook his many
shortcomings: his spells in prison, his numerous nefarious
escapades, his scrapes with other smiths and sculptors, 'his
homicides and brawls'. But what in particular draws Fleur – and
Muriel – to him is his love of art and his fidelity to his calling.

One day, muses Fleur, determined to follow in his gilded footsteps, 'I'll write the tale of my life. But first I have to live.'

These were also Muriel's thoughts. Her life may not have been as eventful and turbulent as Cellini's, but it was not without its own *Sturm und Drang* and deserved to be recorded, if only to demonstrate how a girl from a family of slender means emerged from a relatively small and introverted city on the periphery of Europe to become a writer of international renown, a critical as well as a commercial success. In a very real sense Muriel's life is to be found in her work. She always said that if anyone wanted to know about the person behind the prose and poems they had only to read them closely and imaginatively. She is there, in the times and places and characters, in the way she uses language, in the choice of words and the construction of sentences, in the tone of voice, above all in the philosophy of existence. Whenever I want to hear her speak I open a page at random of any of her novels and there she is, loud and clear, note perfect.

To read *Loitering With Intent*, which is narrated in the first person, is like listening to her give testimony on a day of judgement. In common with her creator, Fleur Talbot has had to struggle to make herself heard. Trained, like Muriel, to be a secretary, she is a meticulous maintainer of order and an assiduous filer of papers, because she believes that in the future they might be of interest to someone. This in itself is telling. Who keeps such records if they do not believe themselves to be in some way special? Years after the scene in the graveyard, Fleur riffles through her papers and comes across a final demand from a bookseller asking urgently for payment to be made for books bought. Failure to do so means that 'further steps' will be taken. She is disturbed by what exactly this could entail, as was Muriel, who in the late 1940s and early 1950s often received such injunctions and who had been brought up to live in dread of debt. 'I remember at the time thinking the letter about the further steps quite funny and worth keeping,' Fleur reflects. 'Perhaps I wrote and told them that I was quite terrified of their steps approaching, further, nearer, nearer; perhaps I didn't actually write this but only considered doing so. Apparently I paid them in the end for the final receipt is there, £5.8.9.'

Here, in this brief passage, is an example in microcosm of how Muriel turned life into art. Books were bought and bills went unpaid until such time as they could no longer be ignored. That much is verifiable. Where fiction takes over is in Fleur's reaction to the ominous stock phrase 'further steps'. Poverty-stricken Muriel may well have been terrified of their approach. But did she write to the bookseller articulating her fear? Most probably not. In *Loitering With Intent*, Fleur, who will shortly publish her debut novel, is struck by how much easier it is to deal with imaginary characters than real ones. Muriel has her narrator explain: 'In a novel the author invents characters and arranges them in convenient order. Now that I come to write biographically I have to tell of whatever actually happened and whoever naturally turns up. The story of a life is a very informal party; there are no rules of precedence and hospitality, no invitations.'

In 1981 Muriel was not yet ready to allow a biographer to perform an autopsy on her. Perhaps she felt, like Saul Bellow, that his or her arrival would cast 'the shadow of the tombstone' across her life. Nor was she inclined to consider writing a memoir or an autobiography for that would suggest that the well of creativity was drying up and that there was nothing left for her to do but plunder her past. But as she grew older her attitude changed and she realised that, no matter how she might feel about it, her head, like that of an outlaw sought by bounty hunters, had a price on it and that sooner or later she would be captured and brought to book. It was not a happy prospect. Though she liked to read biographies, the idea of being the subject of one was not something she looked forward to. She was not at all keen, for instance, on the kind of biography that 'adheres relentlessly to fact, faithfully recounting all that undoubtedly happened and nothing that perhaps happened . . .' Writing about other people's lives, as she knew from her own experience of immersing herself in the lives of John Masefield, the Brontës and Mary Shelley, was inherently frustrating and destined ultimately to be unsatisfactory. It was like fishing. Just when you think you're about to land an elusive fish it wriggles off the hook and disappears into the deep from whence it came. No life can be wholly recaptured in words. Something is always missing or unnecessarily included, or over-emphasised, or mis-recalled or made more of, or less of, than it merits. Scott Fitzgerald said that there never could be a good biography of a good novelist, because if he is any good he is too many people; Muriel would certainly have agreed with him.

It came as something of a surprise, therefore, when in 1992, she wrote to tell me that she had agreed to allow Martin Stannard, a professor of Modern English Literature at the University of Leicester, to be her biographer and that she had given him 'official' status. I thought it an odd moment to make such a critical decision, because earlier that year she had published her first volume of autobiography. Another, she teased in its closing lines, would be forthcoming. *Curriculum Vitae* ends in 1957 with the publication of *The Comforters*, Muriel's debut novel, which came garlanded with praise from Graham Greene ('one of the few really original novels one has read in years') and Evelyn Waugh ('brilliantly original and fascinating').

Curriculum Vitae is an evocative, elegantly written book, which disappointed some reviewers who felt that it lacked revelations though it contains plenty if you look hard enough. Muriel sent me a proof copy, in part to see whether we would like to run an extract in the *Scotsman* (which we did) and also to check it for factual slips. One passage puzzled me, as it does still. Writing about Miss Christina Kay, her inspirational teacher, Muriel said that she did not know why in *The Prime of Miss Jean Brodie* she chose to name Miss Kay's alter ego Miss Brodie. Recently, however, she had learned that another teacher, Charlotte Rule, who had taught her to read in infant school, had been a Miss Brodie before her marriage. 'Could I have heard this fact and recorded it unconsciously?' Well, I suppose she could have. But it was surely more likely, as I pointed out, that Miss Brodie took her name from the infamous William 'Deacon' Brodie who, in eighteenth-century Edinburgh, led a respectable life by day as a carpenter and a freeman of the city and who, when night fell, thieved from the premises to which his official position gave him access, for which he duly hanged. If Muriel believed this theory to be valid she never said and there the matter rested.

Martin Stannard had written a biography of Evelyn Waugh which Muriel had read for review and admired. He wrote to thank her and received in reply a letter in which Muriel said that, come the right moment, she hoped she might be lucky enough to have such a good book written about her. Taking this as a hint, Stannard offered his services, which Muriel impulsively accepted. Perhaps she thought that nothing would ultimately come of it: her friend Gore Vidal entrusted his own 'sacred story' to a journalist who spent nearly a decade working on it without producing so much as a page. If she thought that, she was mistaken. Like so many famous writers, she came to regret her rashness. By signing a contract she had given someone she barely knew her blessing to poke around in her past, to interview her friends (and enemies), and to rummage in her private papers. With hindsight, it was an astonishingly reckless act by a woman who was normally so circumspect. What, I often thought, had possessed her, given the years of angst and anxiety it induced? Muriel may have felt that she had the power of veto over whatever her biographer produced. Or she may, as Stannard hazarded in the preface to his book, published three years after her death, have been bored with writing about herself and simply wanted someone to do the job for her. 'Was this', he wondered, 'a way of putting her literary house in order, leaving her remaining years free for creation?'

The irony of this would not be missed by Muriel who spent many of those fragile years locked in dispute with her self-appointed Nemesis. Whole days were lost as she and Penny attempted to answer his lengthy inquiries. This was her reward for telling Stannard that he should treat her as though she was dead. But she was a far cry from drawing her last breath and the deeper Stannard dug and the more hours she spent responding to his questions, in person and by fax, the more she began to resent his presence and regret her decision to give him unfettered access to her. It was an unfortunate coincidence that his name bore such a euphonic resemblance to that of Derek Stanford, the disciple who turned out to be her Judas. Muriel was well into her eighties when a copy of Stannard's manuscript arrived for her inspection and approval. To say she was not amused is to test the meaning of 'understatement'. On one of my many visits, as we sat at the kitchen table, she would read out errant passages in the manner of a schoolteacher-of-old heaping scorn on the effort of a witless pupil. If it was up to her, she said, it would never be published, and she did whatever she could to stall its publication. She handed me the copy to see for myself the extent to which she found fault with it. The typescript was like a battlefield: spattered with corrections and deletions, explanations and interpolations, underlinings and rewriting. Page after page looked as if it had been ink-bombed. Not a word the biographer had written pleased her. Above all, she did not recognise the person portrayed. Who was this woman who seemed never to have cracked a joke in her life or been the recipient of a positive review? Whoever it was, it was not her. To comfort her I quoted Burns – 'O wad some Power the giftie gie us / To see oursels as ithers see us!' – but I might as well have poured salt in the wound for all the good it did.

In September, 2003, when Muriel was eighty-five, she wrote to say that she and Penny were desperate to leave the 'Gran Caldo' – great heat – of Tuscany for cooler climes. There had been no rain since April and everything in the garden, 'stout oak trees' included, had perished. She had received a couple of invitations which would permit them to make their escape. First, they were heading for Grignan – 'the home of Madame de Sévigné's daughter' – where there was to be a round table discussion on the subject of British women writers. After that they would be travelling east through the Jura to Colmar with the aim of seeing the Isenheim Altar – 'one of the major destinations of both our lives' – and then on via Strasbourg, Nuremberg and Marienbad to Prague. It was a journey of some 1,350 miles, all to be driven by Penny in the purring Alfa. This was of no consequence to either of them. On the contrary, they loved, like Thelma and Louise, to be on the move. Muriel, Penny wrote, was in the process of packing. 'It seems to be a very creative process.' They would reach Prague on 6 October where they were due to stay for a week. 'Penelope says why don't you join us there?' added Muriel. 'I will be working for the British Council a bit, not too much, and for my publisher, just, I think, talking to students and posing for my photo. It would be good to have pals with us. We'd love it.'

A week or so later Penny faxed details of the hotel in which they were to be put up but on looking closer at the correspondence she discovered that the promised information from the British Council had not turned up. 'They do seem to be somewhat influenced by Kafka,' she wrote. 'What other Czech writers should we know?' In my reply I mentioned Ivan Klima, with whom I had once played football when we were both at the Harbourfront Writers' Festival in Toronto. As it happened, Klima had been invited to a lunch in Muriel's honour by the British ambassador in Prague. It was agreed that we would meet at the five-star Intercontinental where they would be staying and which, according to its own publicity, had 'three designated non-smoking floors and one room specially designed for disabled guests'. I decided these were facilities I could do without and found a room – a cell might be a more accurate term – in a small and much more modest establishment. What I didn't know at the time was that in the basement it hosted a jazz club which began to jump when I felt the need to sleep.

On Muriel's recommendation I took with me a copy of George Simenon's novel *Black Rain*. 'It is wonderful. I wish there were some new good writers like Simenon coming up. But there are not. I get sent heaps of books. I read the beginning and a bit of the middle and that's enough.' Prague was cold and wet. On the bus from the airport to the Old Town Square I was identified as an ignorant tourist with criminal tendencies by a leather-jacketed, fur-collared inspector who took one look at my ticket, saw that I had neglected to validate it and decided I should be ejected or fined or have a fingernail or two extracted. At least that's what I think she was saying. The bus was crowded and while the inspector and I duelled in mutual miscomprehension my fellow passengers stared into space or at their newspapers as we all do when determined not to get involved in other people's misfortune. Eventually, the inspector realised the futility of interrogating someone whose response was to show her the palms of his hands and shrug his shoulders, and backed off. When I relayed all this to Muriel her response was: 'Couldn't you have just taken a taxi?'

The programme designed by the British Council was not onerous. The morning after I arrived Muriel gave a reading to philosophy students at Charles University, none of whom, it seemed, was conversant with English. A translator did his best to keep up with her but the students looked puzzled, as if they had no idea who she was and why they had been brought to meet her. Later that afternoon there was a signing, organised by Muriel's Czech publisher, at the Fišer Bookstore on Kaprova Street, opened in 1933 but which, alas, has since closed. The bookstore's busy staff seemed somewhat surprised to see us; it was as if we were guests who had turned up a day early for a dinner party. No one from Muriel's publisher was there to greet us or make introductions. Apparently, Muriel's arrival had coincided with the Frankfurt Book Fair, hence the lack of fanfare. We browsed for a while and Muriel signed a few books, then we left, muttering darkly. Lunch the following day at the

British Embassy helped cheer us up. We shared a lift with Ivan Klima, who smiled a lot and spoke sparingly. Our host, the British ambassador, was Glasgow-born Anne Pringle, a self-styled 'rock chick' who in London had once been a near-neighbour of Mick Jagger. She later became the ambassador to Moscow. Muriel's final official obligation was an afternoon reading at Solidni Nejistota cafe which, because of her publisher's neglect, was notable for the near-absence of an audience. In the midst of it appeared an elderly man with an Old Testament beard and a lunatic gaze, who had attached to his coat such an array of knives, forks and spoons that he rattled when he made the slightest movement. Muriel looked bemused, as well she might, peering through her big glasses at a scene that summed up the chaotic nature of our visit.

This was the Prague of Kafka, a city of the absurd and fantastical, where things were never quite as expected and were unlikely to go to plan. On our last night we took a box at the State Opera and sipped champagne that was as cheap as it was cheering. The opera was *Die Zauberflöte* and the performance, by the resident company, was thrilling. In the middle of it a mobile phone rang and I was ready to throttle its inconsiderate owner until I recognised it as mine. In the dark I had trouble locating it, as it rang and rang and rang while Tamino and Papageno struggled to maintain their vow of silence. If Muriel and Penny heard it they did not let on. When we emerged into the night the heavens had opened and opera goers competed to hail a cab. While others dallied I managed to requisition one that had probably been prebooked and we three sped off towards a restaurant that had been recommended by a journalist colleague who said it was the one place in Prague where dumplings were not ubiquitous.

Alexander Moffat's portrait of Muriel Spark, which hangs in
the Scottish National Portrait Gallery

It proved a perfect choice. Buoyed by the opera and by our swift exit Muriel was in a mood to celebrate. As the wine flowed I broached the possibility of her attending the Edinburgh International Book Festival which would be celebrating its twenty-first birthday in August of the following year. She had never been before, which seemed incomprehensible. Although she had been a regular visitor to her homeland over the years, and had visited to have her portrait painted by Alexander Moffat for the National Portrait Gallery, the general public had no access to her on those occasions. She was not getting any younger. On and on I burbled, not knowing what her reaction might be. I did know that of all the significant places in her life Edinburgh was the most problematic for her, principally because of the rift with her son Robin. But during that evening in Prague, these concerns seemed to be of little consequence. Muriel talked warmly of her childhood and of the Edinburgh of the 1920s and 30s, of her schooling and school friends, of the indelible mark the city of her birth and early upbringing had left on her. As she spoke she could have been just another Morningside dame taking afternoon tea in Jenners, looking out across Princes Street to the Scott Monument and Castle Rock and the craggy skyline of the Old Town. 'All right,' she said, 'I will go to Edinburgh next August.'

It was snowing in the Val di Chiana. Muriel's eighty-sixth birthday was imminent and I had come to participate in the celebrations. Penny had hoped to meet me at Arezzo station, as she had done countless times before, but the snow had not melted and she and Muriel were housebound. It was bitterly cold and the *Aretini* moved cautiously, like neophyte ice-skaters. There was no alternative but to book into the Continentale and pray that overnight there would be a thaw. Fat chance. Late the next morning I called a taxi and was dropped at Oliveto, half a mile or so from San Giovanni. No one was about. All around the fields were covered in snow. The smell of woodsmoke was in the air. A gun went off and a dog yelped as if someone had stepped on a paw. The snow, said Penny, as she unbolted the front door, had come suddenly, an industrial amount falling in a few hours. I found Muriel in her study, up the stone staircase, across the treacherous, polished tiles, through shuttered rooms lined with paintings and insulated with books.

The Finishing School, her twenty-second novel, had recently been published and we talked about it for a while. Set in Switzerland, it was about a peripatetic school with a mere eight students. College Sunrise is run largely by Rowland Manor and his wife. Rowland wants to be a writer but he has a rival in one of his students, Chris Wiley, a precocious teenager who has written a novel about Mary, Queen of Scots, and the murders of her Italian secretary David Rizzio and her husband Lord Darnley, who was party to the murder of Rizzio. Some historians believe that Mary may have had a hand in Darnley's subsequent murder but Chris has another theory. He thinks that Jacopo Rizzio, David's brother, could have murdered Darnley in an act of fraternal revenge.

'Jacopo was brought to Edinburgh by David,' Muriel said, sitting behind her large, paraphernalia-strewn desk. 'He was mentioned as a possible member of a gang who killed Darnley on a public, but anonymous, poster of the time. But the idea was soon dropped in the effort to provide a more important political motive for the murder. I have thought it strange that, human nature being what it is, Jacopo was not the natural and immediate suspect. The brother of an Italian murdered basely, as was Rizzio, in the Renaissance days would be almost bound to vindicate his death. I really do believe this aspect of Mary, Queen of Scots' story has been overlooked. I have only touched on it in my novel as a valid theme.'

Her continued interest in Mary was a reminder of her Edinburgh antecedents. She recalled how, some seventy years previously, she had visited the palace of Holyrood as a young and impressionable girl, escorted by Christina Kay, as the girls of Marcia Blaine's would have been by Miss Brodie. Muriel was particularly taken, she recalled, by the size of Mary's bed which, for someone who was 'billed as a tall queen', she felt was 'too short'. It taught her never to take any information for granted and always to ask questions no matter how obvious the answer may seem. As the snow continued to fall, Muriel, nursing a medicinal tincture of whisky, was in a pensive mood. 'With hindsight, which is a wonderful thing, I could rewrite my life entirely,' she said. 'I can see motives that I couldn't see at the time for having done things. I can see very good motives, very good reasons, why I acted as I did. Generally speaking, I must say I approve of what I did. I often look back and think, 'Should I have done that?' I think, 'Given the circumstance, yes, I should.' And also, you know, looking back – if one must look back – it's sometimes good to look back – one can over-simplify.'

We spent the afternoon with Penny in the kitchen, eating, drinking, talking, eyes smarting from a fire fed on wet olive branches. Muriel talked about the art of writing, how when she came to write a novel it was not what it was about that truly interested her. Rather, her main focus was the characters, their actions and reactions, and their dialogue. I had recently been to

Alan Taylor with Muriel at her study in San Giovanni. 'The difficulty of starting a book is getting the tone'

America where I had interviewed Joseph Heller who told me he could not begin writing a novel until he had found the perfect first sentence, which could take years.

'The difficulty of starting a book is getting the tone,' Muriel acknowledged. 'It's like tuning up. It's very like music, a book, you know. You really have to have a balance, a rhythm. First of all, are you going to tell it in the first person? And what sort of sympathy are you going to attract? If you want to attract a lot of sympathy to a character, the first person is unbeatable. If you're telling it in the third person, then who are you? You're not really the author. My name's Muriel Spark and it's not that. This is another character in the novel telling the story: the narrator. And you have to decide on what type of character. What their values are, and from what point of view. And to get that across to the reader.'

The Finishing School, by its very title, seemed to sound a valedictory note, as did its closing lines, which were lifted from the weather forecast on Sky News, which Muriel never missed: 'as we go through this evening and into tonight'. I wondered if she had intended to send such a message. Was this to be her last novel? 'Well, I thought it probably would be,' she said. 'Maybe it is. When you get to be eighty-six you realise you've got to die some time. But I feel very healthy. I don't have a great deal of memory trouble. No mental problems. I do everything at half pace, except think. I wasn't thinking I was ready for death and to die yet. In fact I was thinking after I finished *The Finishing School* I might not take on a novel again. I was very tired. I thought maybe I could do short stories. Then I got ready for a novel again. I felt lonely without a novel on the desk, so I started on one.'

She smiled. I felt, then, as the embers glowed and pellets of hail dropped down the chimney and fell hissing on to the hearth, that death was all that could come between Muriel and her work. It was what she had always wanted to do and nothing and no one could stop her except her own unpredictable health. In *The Finishing School* she has Rowland speak for her: 'If, in the course of an author's preparing a book, his family suffers a blow or a tragedy, the book can easily come to ruin in the ensuing domestic anguish and muddle. The average author can no doubt finish the book, but not well. However, the dedicated author might seem callous, not easily shattered, tough. Hence the reputation of artists in all fields for ruthless, cold detachment. Too bad. About this sort of accusation the true artist is uncaring. The true artist is almost unaware of other people's care and distractions. This applies to either sex.'

Over the next few months I kept in regular contact with Muriel, not wanting her enthusiasm for her appearance at the book festival in Edinburgh to wane. Catherine Lockerbie, its then director, felt that it was 'the single most wonderful thing' that could happen in its coming-of-age year and promised to do whatever was needed to make it a reality. In March, Muriel and I had a rehearsal at the Queen Elizabeth Hall in London, which augured well. By the summer, however, she was feeling anxious about the prospect. 'I am beginning to get cold feet about the flutter and fuss of the festival,' she wrote in July, 'and have no idea whatsoever what my role is to be. Can you write and assure me that you will negotiate, initiate and introduce my proceedings so that I can answer and invite questions and that will, I hope, set me off. Do say Yes and put me out of my misery.'

She had been asked by the organisers to nominate a writer she believed had been forgotten and chose T. F. Powys, author of *Mr Weston's Good Wine*. 'Penelope', she added, 'thinks he is not forgotten, however. Here in Tuscany we are all forgotten. It is the beautiful nature of our lives.' She was having trouble with her eyes and could only read large print. She wanted reassurance about the lighting and wondered where she might stay before her arrival in Edinburgh. I suggested she and Penny spend a night or two at Burt's Hotel in Melrose, a few miles from Abbotsford, the pile built by Sir Walter Scott even as he struggled to repay his debtors, where it was agreed I would join them. 'Please don't tell anyone we are there,' pleaded Muriel.

No sooner had she arrived in Melrose than she discovered the local bookshop which was owned by a distant relative of mine. She had bought a few books, one of which she couldn't put down. It was one, she said, that she'd been looking for all her life. She produced a brick-sized tome. It was published by Reader's Digest and titled *How To Do Just About Anything*: deal with a gas leak, prune roses, repair a zip, change a tyre, extricate yourself from quicksand, the kind of practical advice, she said, which every novelist ought ideally to have to hand. Over supper in the hotel bar we discussed how best to fill the hour at the festival. Muriel wanted to read from a short story, 'The Girl I Left Behind Me', *The Finishing School*, *The Prime* and some poems. I felt this would eat too much into the allotted time, a fair proportion of which was scheduled to be given over to questions from the audience. In the end Muriel agreed to read two short extracts from *The Prime* and a couple of poems. 'I'm in your hands,' she said, adroitly delegating responsibility.

The 600 tickets had sold within a couple of hours of going on sale. Apparently, some tickets had changed hands for as much as £100, about ten times their face value. 'All Edinburgh', a *Guardian* reporter wrote, 'had been fighting tooth-and-claw for a seat.' Wearing a caramel-coloured trouser suit and walking tentatively with the aid of a stick, Muriel entered the teeming tent to a spontaneous, standing ovation. As she began to read, her voice firm and nerveless, her accent familiarly local, one could sense that the audience was willing her on and that they were witness to an occasion unlikely ever to be repeated. When the applause abated Muriel took as her text a passage from *The Prime of Miss Jean Brodie*, reading slowly and with a pause for dramatic emphasis: 'If only you small girls would listen to me I would make of you the crème de la crème.' This was what everyone had come to hear and they were not disappointed. Many of them seemed to have the sentences off by heart and lip-read along with her. Here was Muriel Spark in person, the native returned, witty, waspish, a wonder to behold, the true crème de la crème, reiterating more than once when quizzed about her 'exile' in Italy: 'I consider Edinburgh as my home.'

DAME MURIEL SPARK

Memorial Concert

Tuesday 17 April 2007 at 7.30pm

The programme for Muriel's Memorial Concert at the Wigmore Hall, London, in 2007

ENVOI

And so, having entered the fullness of my years, from there
by the grace of God I go on my way rejoicing.
LOITERING WITH INTENT

The last communication I had with Muriel was towards the end of January 2006. My wife Rene and I had separated and Muriel wrote to express her sadness and to wish us both well. 'These things', she added, 'are entirely a matter of one's choice.' As for herself and Penny the news, like the weather, was mixed. 'We work very hard,' Muriel wrote, 'but I have been in hospital where they took away a dud kidney and its foul attachment. I feel I have a hole in my body, but as I will be 88 next week I feel glad that I got through it all without complications. I am home now. We have a good GP here and a nurse. I have lost my reading sight but we have acquired a new reading machine which is beautiful.'

She had been asked by Barbara Epler of New Directions, her American publisher, to write an introduction to Vladimir Nabokov's *The Real Life of Sebastian Knight*, a biography of his half-brother. It seemed an unnecessary commission to take on at this point. Nor did it look as if she was making much headway with it. She was 'trying' to write it, she said, which did not suggest it was proceeding at a lick. 'You will have to come and see us as it is such a performance for us to move,' she concluded, 'although we are hoping for a holiday in the spring.' The letter was typed by Penny and signed off 'Love' by Muriel. It was the last word she wrote to me.

On the Easter weekend I was travelling with my partner, Rosemary Goring, to the Wigtown Book Festival in the south-west corner of Scotland when I received a call from the BBC. I knew – how I know not – before the reporter on the other end spoke that it concerned Muriel and that it was to tell me she had died. Would I care to make a comment? I muttered the first few sentences that came into my head and then began to wonder how I could possibly get to Italy in time for her funeral.

At Biggar in the Borders we pulled over and I managed to get a signal and phoned Penny on her mobile. She sounded awfully far away and was too bereft to talk for long. Muriel had died of cancer two days earlier in Florence, on the thirteenth of April, the eve of Good Friday, with Penny at her bedside. She was in no pain and had made her peace with her Maker. She had surely known for some time that she did not have long to live but never spoke of it. At the hospital, before she fell into a coma, a priest arrived to take her confession. She must not have had much to confess, said Penny, because he spent only a few minutes with her.

After the formalities had been completed her body had been returned to Oliveto for the funeral service and burial. I had caught Penny just as she was leaving San Giovanni for the obsequies. Her trusty friend, Airdrie Armstrong Terenghi, who lives in nearby Poggibonsi where she runs the Linari classical music festival, had arranged for a Dutch trio to play. There would be Schubert and Beethoven by way of consolation. The line was bad and so we rang off, promising to be in touch as soon as was practicable.

As a Catholic Muriel believed in an afterlife. But even someone with her fertile imagination could not picture what it might actually be like. The 'next world', as she termed it, was a place, though much written of, that nobody knows a thing about. She had often longed to go there, she said, as if it were Azerbaijan or Zhangzhou, so that she could come back and write a book about it. Heaven interested her but only as it might a thrill-seeking tourist. Long-term residency did not appeal. She preferred 'pagan outsiders', like Aristotle, Virgil and Socrates, to 'good souls', such as the American evangelist Billy Graham. She also thought it would be too noisy, what with the beating of angels' wings and other celestial bugbears. Even in paradise she would need peace to work. 'As for Hell,' she wrote, 'there is no visiting that place. To my mind it is the essential void. "Hell is empty," cries Ferdinand in *The Tempest*, "and all the devils are here." With that, few would disagree.'

Rosemary and I had several hours to go before we reached Wigtown. It is a route I have always liked, deep in the debatable lands of southern Scotland with the English border never far away. Cars are few and sheep many. The hills are those in which the reivers wreaked havoc and over which Richard Hannay in John Buchan's 'shocker', *The Thirty-Nine Steps*, sought to evade his pursuers. Richard Walker, the editor of the *Sunday Herald*, managed to get hold of me and asked if I would like to write a tribute to Muriel.

I spent the rest of the journey fielding more calls and composing what I might say. My thoughts turned to our first appointment in Arezzo all those years ago, on that hot and humid summer evening when the light was fading fast and Muriel gave the photographer a mere ten minutes in which to do his job. In those days I met many writers. None made the impression on me Muriel did. None had her aura. She felt both familiar and mysterious, so Scottish yet also so foreign. Our rapport, our affinity, was enhanced by a shared sense of humour and similar roots. 'Blood speaking to blood?' as Penny put it all those years ago.

Penny knew her better than anyone yet even she used occasionally to say, 'Sometimes I think I never knew Muriel at all.' I think I know what she meant. There was an ethereal, unearthly, elusive air to Muriel. With her piercing blue eyes, red hair, porcelain-pale skin and elfin frame she could appear doll-like. There was a tendency, too, for her to alter the way she looked, by changing how her hair had been done or the clothes she had chosen to wear or the weight she had gained or lost. Some old friends felt that there were many Muriels, that she was a chameleon, modifying her appearance to suit her surroundings as she moved from one place to another. But at her core Muriel was immutable. From her first breath to her last she embodied the values instilled in her when she was growing up in Scotland. When she said she was 'Scottish by formation' she meant just that. She was speaking literally, not metaphorically. Those youthful years had shaped her to a degree that she herself could barely comprehend. She was a compound of many elements: time, place, people, genes, education, reading, religion, climate, bricks and mortar. Everything was material: the food she had eaten, the friends and neighbours she saw daily, the conversations she overheard, the cries in the street, the games she played.

In *Curriculum Vitae*, in a chapter headed 'Myths and Images', Muriel remembered as a small girl in the early 1920s sitting at the window waiting at the dimming of the day for the lamp-lighter to come and turn on the gas lamps with his long pole. It was her umbilical connection with Robert Louis Stevenson, who died in 1894, and his poems, gathered in *A Child's Garden of Verses*, which was one of the first books she owned. There were no writers in her own family, and Stevenson became a mentor, one whose example she must follow. 'I felt a close affinity with our long-dead Edinburgh writer', she wrote, 'on the basis of more than one shared experience. The Braid Hills, the Blackford Hill and Pond, the Pentland Hills of Stevenson's poems, his "hills of home", were mine, too.'

Like Stevenson, Muriel was an enthusiastic socialiser. Like him, too, she would be one of the first names on any dinner party list. But she was also, like him, self-contained, wrapped up in her work, determined never to be deflected from the task at hand. She knew that this could be hard for others to accept but there was nothing she could do about it. It came with the job. Unlike so many other people, Penny, as an artist herself, understood and tolerated this. For her part, Muriel felt that she may have affected Penny's chances of marriage, which Penny insisted was not the case. Interviewed by Stephen Schiff for the *New Yorker*, Muriel said: 'Penelope loves to be with me. We're very fond of each other, you know. We're not lesbians, but we're very fond of each other. After my marriage ended I never met anybody I wanted to marry who was free to marry me or wanted to marry me. Besides, you know, you're only half there if you're a writer. Men used to complain that I was only half there and wasn't listening. But I am listening. Sometimes I reflect on what people are saying, and it gives me an absent appearance.'

When Rosemary and I arrived at the cottage in which we were staying at Wigtown I wrote quickly about the Muriel I knew, whose work I loved as much as I did her. What I wanted to convey was her sense of fun and her ferocious artistic ambition; in every respect she had lived life to the full. She had put her all into it. She may have been a convert to Roman Catholicism, I noted, but her work ethic was Calvinist. In her, the cold, grey, porridgy northern light clashed with the blinding sunshine and citrus shades of the south. Leaving Scotland gave her licence to be glamorous, to embrace colour. It also allowed her to take risks and to follow her instinct which in Edinburgh, that most cautious of cities, was frowned upon. I thought it worth mentioning, too, that when critics referred to her they rarely mentioned other writers with whom she might be compared or who influenced her stylistically. Unlike Stevenson, she never played the 'sedulous ape' to anyone. Rather than imitate she was determined to improve as she did when, still at school, she took the work of famous poets and rewrote it. It never occurred to her that this might be viewed as disrespectful or presumptuous; it was simply something that she did for her own amusement, and because she could. The books she re-read, she said, were few. First, there was *A La Recherche du Temps Perdu* and then there was the Bible, especially the Old Testament, which she recommended to students of creative writing. The books she could never re-read were her own, copies of which she tended to keep out of sight. 'It's not that they embarrass me intellectually,' she said. 'I just don't want to relive those books at all.'

My deadline approached. What images returned? I remembered once, when in the car on our way to lunch at Cortona or Orvieto, Muriel and I were talking about the Border ballads and she began to recite 'Twa Corbies', a poem that as a child always made my flesh creep. It tells of a slain knight whose body has been left to rot behind a dyke. His lady has left him for another lover and his hawk and hound are nowhere to be seen. To the corbies – ravens or crows – the knight is carrion. They peck out his eyes and tear away at his hair which they will use to build a nest. It is a brutal, bloody poem:

As I was walking all alane,
I heard twa corbies makin a mane;
The tane unto the ither did say-O,
'Whar sall we gang and dine the-day-O?'

What Muriel admired about the ballads was their 'steel and bite'. She read them so often, she said, that she memorised them without noticing it. They were 'so remorseless and yet so lyrical' and entered her literary bloodstream, 'never to depart'.

The ballads gave her from an early age a taste of the macabre, which, likewise, never left her. She and Penny shared an enthusiasm for a good murder, the more lurid and juicy and mysterious the better. They were intrigued, for example, to learn that I had once spent an evening with the Florence-based crime writer Magdalen Nabb, who in 1996 had written a novel called *The Monster of Florence*, inspired by the seven double homicides that took place between 1968 and 1985 in and around the Tuscan capital. Nabb was better informed than most through her connections with the *carabinieri*. Muriel was envious. She was always on the lookout for similar cases that might provide the backdrop to a novel and she would scour the Italian papers for tales of terror and titillation, which she would cut out and keep for possible future use.

Once she told me of the 'chilling and puzzling' story of an Italian family, composed of a widowed middle-aged mother and her three adult sons, who all together one morning had thrown themselves over a viaduct on the Rome–Aquila autostrada. Apparently they had been seen earlier that morning parked in an emergency lay-by by a police patrol car. Asked what the matter was the eldest son said that his mother was feeling unwell so they had stopped for a minute to allow her to recover. When later in the day the police returned to the same spot they found the car doors flung wide open and four bodies lying in close proximity on the ground far below, which seemed to point to the family having jumped hand in hand.

This intrigued Muriel who, I felt, would have made a perfect Poirot or Miss Marple. A psychiatrist, she said, speculated that there was a 'high charge' of depression in the family, whose dominant member was the mother. Debt may have been another factor. A sum of a million dollars was mentioned as being owed which, Muriel suggested, they could have worked to pay off had they been motivated. After all, the sons were not ill-educated. Instead they had opted to commit suicide. It was what Muriel called 'the fatal sickness of any hope, the death of any future'. They may well have been facing bankruptcy, but so what? Why kill yourself for that? For Muriel this represented 'the respectable bourgeois mentality at its most pathetic'. What fools the four had been, what absolute fools.

The Finishing School turned out to be Muriel's last novel. I learned later from Penny that in her last months – as she said she would – she had embarked on another. Perhaps she thought she could defy the odds and live long enough to see it through to completion. A few days before she died she told an admirer who was based in India, 'I have to believe that everything is possible.' She was referring specifically to her work but, who knows, she may have felt that miracles do happen and that she was due one.

She gave the novel she had started a provisional title: *Destiny*. It concerned the scandal associated with Roberto Calvi, nicknamed 'God's Banker'. In 1982, Calvi was found hanging from scaffolding beneath Blackfriars Bridge in London. His clothing was stuffed with bricks and he was carrying a

literary estate and tends to San Giovanni and its half acre of land. She is still planting olive trees which will continue to fruit long into the future. In the part of the house that is reserved for guests, Muriel's presence remains palpable. There is one of her several sets of the *Encyclopeadia Britannica*, box upon box stuffed with her papers, a wardrobe full of her clothes. We sit in the kitchen as we did in years gone by. Only now we talk not about the war in Iraq or what the effect of Scottish independence might be or Piero's enduring genius but of Muriel, of what she would think of this or that. Penny has a new and formidably modern stove which Muriel, who 'just about knew how to open a tin of sardines', would have had nothing to do with. Would she have even known how to turn it on? I rather doubt it.

Most days we take the car and tour familiar haunts – Castello di Gargonza, Monterchi, Sansepolcro, Anghiari, Pienza, Monterchi, Arezzo – as if they are Stations of the Cross. One day Penny offered to drive to Urbino to view Piero's *Flagellation*, but the round trip would take at least seven hours, probably more. Another time perhaps, another reason to return, as if one is needed. Instead we might go to Cortona or, if time is short, Monte San Savino or Castiglion Fiorentino, where the ever-industrious Vasari built a nine-arched loggia. There is no end of things to do. On every visit, as shadows lengthen, I stroll down the *strada bianca* towards somnolent Oliveto where if you're lucky a familiar face will look up from his raking or hoeing and bid you '*buona sera*'. A few hundred yards from San Giovanni the road forks. To the left is the village's crowded walled cemetery. As is typical in Italy, many of the graves are adorned with snapshots. Muriel's nearest neighbour is a man who is remembered not as in the fullness of youth but in his toothless dotage. She is one of the cemetery's few non-natives.

Her stone, placed flat, has no photograph. It has two pots of flowers and a candle. The lettering is weathering already. There is a quote, chosen by Penny, translated into Italian from Muriel's own poem, 'Canaan': 'Not a leaf / Repeats itself, we only repeat the word.' And immediately beneath her name is one simple word, *Poeta*.

ACKNOWLEDGEMENTS

'Acknowledgement' is too weak a word to describe the debts accrued in the writing of this book. Over the years I have met many writers and befriended more than a few but my friendship with Muriel Spark was of a different order. From the outset, we clicked and I never grew weary of reading her work, listening to her talk, receiving her faxes and visiting her in Tuscany. She was always a welcoming and generous host and you had to be on your mettle if you were determined to settle a bill. In all that Muriel did she was most ably aided and abetted by her companion, Penelope Jardine. Penny read my manuscript with insightful care, answered any queries promptly, patiently and wittily, and made many suggestions which were undoubtedly to its benefit. She was Muriel's first reader, and few writers have had a better one. I have often thought that, had she been less modest, Penny would herself have made a wonderful author.

Rosemary Goring, my wife and my own special first reader, has borne with me the pain of confronting a blank page. I fear that without her gentle cajoling and encouraging presence this book would still be 'forthcoming'. I am likewise grateful to James Campbell, a friend of long standing and my editor at the *Times Literary Supplement*, whose skilful and knowledgeable interventions have improved the narrative flow immeasurably. Thanks, too, are due to the members of the small but perfectly formed Muriel Spark Society, which exists to keep the Spark flame alive. I recommend joining it to anyone one who has an interest in Muriel and her oeuvre. May it go on its way rejoicing.

It has been a pleasure to work with Birlinn and various members of its staff: Hugh Andrew, Jim Hutcheson, Kristian Kerr, Anna Marshall, Neville Moir, Vikki Reilly and Jan Rutherford. Special mention, however, must be made of Mairi Sutherland who was instrumental in seeing the book through to completion, including the overcoming of the knotty, sanity-challenging problem of copyright clearance. As the holder of Muriel's vast archive, the National Library of Scotland has been my second home. It is a joy and a privilege to use its facilities and to be able to draw on the expertise of its researchers and keepers, in particular Dr Colin McIlroy, Muriel Spark Project Co-Ordinator; Manuscripts Curator Sally Harrower; Robin Smith, Head of Collections and Research; and Dr John Scally, Chief Executive and National Librarian. Parts of *Appointment in Arezzo* have previously appeared in the following publications, albeit in a much-altered form: *Hidden Possibilities: Essays in Honor of Muriel Spark*, edited by Robert Hosmer (Notre Dame Press, 2014), the *Edinburgh Evening News, Scotland on Sunday,* the *Sunday Herald* and the *Times Literary Supplement.* I salute the editors who commissioned me. All that remains to say is that if there are any errors in this book they are mine, all mine.

PICTURE CREDITS

The publishers are grateful to the following for permission to reproduce photographs on the pages listed:

Sophie Bassouls (p. 78)

Bridgeman Images: The Madonna del Parto, c.1450–70 (fresco) post restoration, Francesca, Piero della (c.1415–92) / Chapel of the Cemetery, Monterchi, Italy (p. 82)

Dan Gunn (pp. 24, 33, 41, 66, 122)

Getty Images: Hulton Archive / Keystone (p. 46); Hulton Archive / Evening Standard (p. 56)

Independent on Sunday / Tom Pilston (pp. 12–13)

National Library of Scotland (pp. 15, 19, 29 © Jerry Bauer, 50, 54, 90 © Jerry Bauer, 109 © Jerry Bauer, 130)

National Portrait Gallery, London / © Mark Gerson (p. 73)

Murdo Macleod (p. 140)

Scottish National Portrait Gallery / © Alexander Moffat. Licensor: www.scran.ac.uk (p. 151)

Shutterstock.com: Michael Avery (p. 6); Belenos (p. 86); Tupungato (p. 104)

Alan Taylor (pp. 126, 155, 160)

University of Tulsa, Tulsa, Oklahoma: Handwritten draft of *The Prime of Miss Jean Brodie* from the Muriel Spark papers, Coll. No. 1983.003, Department of Special Collections and University Archives, McFarlin Library (p. 96)

Every effort has been made to establish copyright and contact copyright holders prior to publication. If contacted, the publishers will be pleased to rectify any omissions or errors at the earliest possible opportunity.